CURVED QUILTING WITH CONFIDENCE

16 MODERN DESIGNS WITH QUARTER-CIRCLE BLOCKS

ANGELA PINGEL

Landauer Publishing

For everyone who has ever cut into fabric with a little fear and a lot of hope.

Curved Quilting with Confidence

Landauer Publishing, *https://landauer.foxchapelpublishing.com*, is an imprint of Fox Chapel Publishing Company, Inc.

Curved Quilting with Confidence contains content first published in *Quilter's Mixology*, published by Interweave.

Project Team
Editorial Director: Brian Hurley
Acquisition Editor: Amelia Johanson
Editor: Madeline DeLuca
Designer: Wendy Reynolds
Photographer: Allison Adams
Technical Editor, Proofreader, and Indexer: Jean Bissell

ISBN 978-1-63981-171-7

Library of Congress Control Number: 2026937852

To learn more about the other great books from Fox Chapel Publishing, or to find a retailer near you, call toll-free 800-457-9112, send mail to 903 Square Street, Mount Joy, PA 17552, or visit us at *www.FoxChapelPublishing.com*.

We are always looking for talented authors. To submit an idea, please send a brief inquiry to acquisitions@foxchapelpublishing.com.

Printed in China
First printing

MIX
Paper | Supporting responsible forestry
FSC® C147414

CONTENTS

INTRODUCTION

Welcome to *Curved Quilting with Confidence*, a book which is a return for me to curved piecing. After over a decade of experience from my curved quilting book on the drunkard's path block and teaching hundreds of people to sew curves, I am still in love with the circle shape. I have brought back my favorite quilts from the original book, *A Quilter's Mixology*, and have updated many of them. But this book is also a place for new designs and patterns using the quarter circle curve. So, I have some wonderful new patterns to share with you as well. What you are getting is the best of the best. Original readers will enjoy the updates to my earlier patterns and the new ones, while readers who have just found me (Welcome!) will be able to access the many patterns that I designed previously but that have been out of print and unavailable. Let's dive in!

JUST THE BASICS

As a former garment sewer, I have never been daunted by sewing curves. In garment sewing, you are lucky to ever actually sew a straight line. This is in strong contrast to sewers who begin their journey with quilting, which can be exclusively straight-line seams. However, if you're new to it, never fear. While the quarter-circle curve (also well known as the Drunkard's Path block) does require curved piecing, in these pages, I'll show you my method for sewing curves with ease. I'll also explain how to cut curved pieces using either an acrylic curve template, the templates provided in this book, or a super-fast die-cutter. You'll be a pro in no time!

This block is made from two basic pieces: a square and a quarter-circle. The square (A) has a concave curve, and the circle (B) has a convex curve. When sewn together with a ¼" (6mm) seam allowance, these pieces become a perfect square.

Note: Before they are sewn, the curves have different diameters, which can be disconcerting when you first look at your templates. But don't worry—they are supposed to be different. They each have a seam allowance added to them. It will all turn out perfectly when you sew them together.

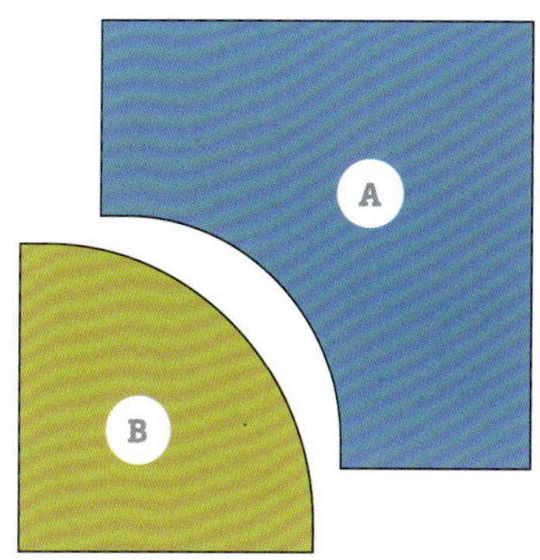

You can arrange a Drunkard's Path block in different ways by rotating blocks and switching the placements of fabrics.

You can arrange quarter-circles in so many different ways to create unique designs.

The classic Drunkard's Path block is made up of pieces that are quarter-circles drafted on squares. You put the pieces together by sewing a concave curve to a convex curve. These blocks can be arranged in many different ways. The classic Drunkard's Path block is shown on page 19. Different settings can be created simply by rotating the blocks and by playing with the placement of dark- and light-value fabrics.

When the quarter-circle shape is broken down and taken apart, it can be turned into something entirely new. It becomes a modern graphic design that reflects the original block but introduces a new vision for using the shape. Some of the designs in this book share elements with traditional variations, while others take off in another direction to create something entirely fresh.

Cat Eye Quilt, page 68

ESSENTIAL TOOLS

Shown here is a standard selection of tools for the modern quilter. If you don't already have these, consider adding them to your personal collection. Get the highest quality you can afford. Basics are fine. You don't need a lot of "bells and whistles," but reliable tools are the first step to successful quilting. Although the sizes of your see-through acrylic rulers are a personal choice, I would recommend having both a long rectangular ruler and a small square ruler.

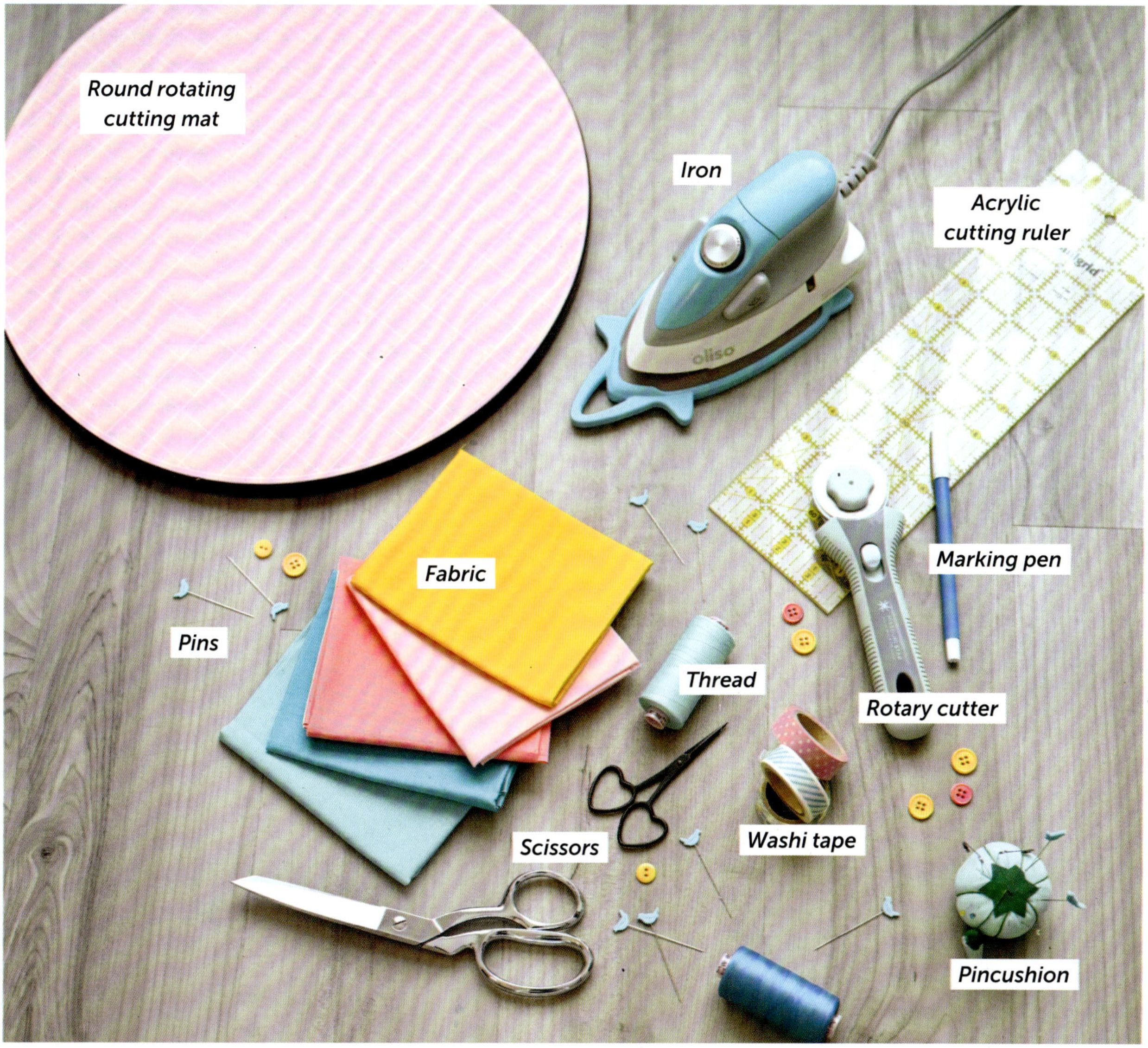

Reliable tools are the first step to successful quilting.

THOUGHTS ON COLOR AND FABRIC

Selecting the fabrics for any project is always a favorite moment in the design process for me. I have what I fondly refer to as a "fabric addiction," which essentially means that I really like fabric: I like to see it, own it, touch it, and use it. There are so many options for fabric designs these days that I would challenge any person in the world not to find a fabric they adore. Like most quilters, I prefer to work with quality, 100 percent cotton fabrics.

FABRIC DESIGN

Sewing curves adds a whole new dimension to selecting fabrics for a quilt design. Cutting curved pieces from fabric patterns gives you a unique opportunity to use directional prints as well as overall patterns. They also lend themselves to fussy-cutting—selecting particular elements in the fabric design to focus on. Directional prints in particular can be your best friend (or your worst enemy) when sewing quarter-circle curves, because you may have to pay attention to four different orientations of a single fabric. But they can be a spectacular showpiece in a quilt as well, providing extra interest simply with the choice of the right fabric.

When choosing prints, consider their scale. Are the fabric patterns large-, medium-, or small-scale? There is no hard-and-fast rule for scale selection, but it should never be ignored. I will often use a mix of fabric scales in a single quilt pattern. But sometimes a pattern can be very specifically geared toward using a particular print of one scale, repeated in several colors as in Paint Drip Quilt (page 52). Very large-scale prints can

Have fun when picking your fabric! Mixing visual textures are very important when planning your design.

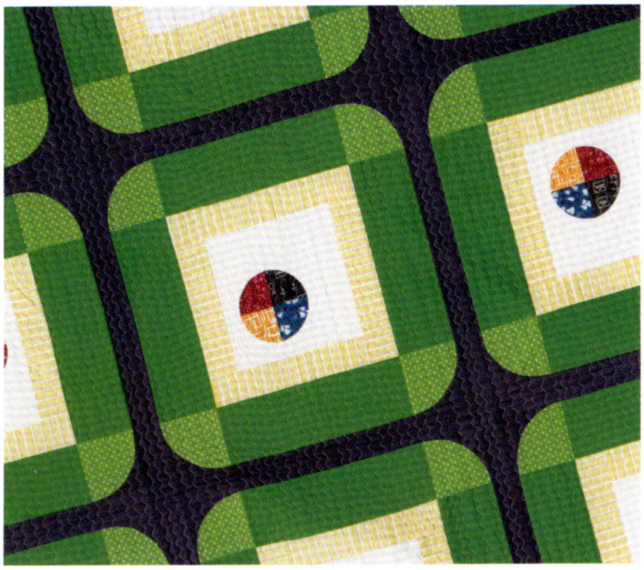

The right fabric can add a pop of bold color to your quilt, like in Tennis Match Quilt (page 40).

I found the background fabric for Full Bloom Quilt (page 80) in the fabric section of the baby store. Expand your mind when searching for fabric.

yield some interesting results when cut into small pieces for a quilt, as in Ornamental Quilt (page 102). Small-scale prints can often read as a solid fabric in a sea of larger-scale prints, as seen in the mini pink polka dot print in Full Bloom Quilt (page 80).

A mixture of visual textures is also important to any design scheme. Text prints look great mixed with modern florals. Or mix a stripe, a reproduction print, a polka dot, and a solid. As with color selection, the right mix of print textures is a personal choice. A quilt may be perfect in all dot prints or all stripes. But most often, a healthy balance of many options will provide the most interest as well as cohesion to your design.

And of course, don't forget to think about incorporating solid fabrics or crossweaves into your fabric selection. (Crossweaves are fabrics like shot cottons and chambrays, which are woven with different colors in the warp and weft so they have special coloration.) Prints are exciting and constantly changing, so it can be easy to overlook the value of creating with all solids or even interspersing solids throughout your project. But solids really are a vital aspect of good fabric selection. They can act as a neutral, providing a resting place for your eyes, as in Arabian Nights Quilt (page 46). Or they can have the opposite effect, acting as a powerful pop of bold color, as seen in Tennis Match Quilt (page 40) and Carnival Quilt (page 114).

Woven solids have no right or wrong side to the fabric, which makes them enormously versatile and easy to use, especially when working with curves. Be careful when working with them, though, because solids also don't hide anything. So, your sewing may need to be a bit more precise.

Also consider blender or low-volume fabric as one of your basics. It can help bridge the gaps between colors and fabrics to create harmony overall. I personally love to use these kinds of fabrics as the entire background for a quilt, as seen in the Temple and Bow Tie pillows (page 26). I have fun hunting in sections of the quilt store that I might not normally go to in order to find fun low-volume prints. Nearly every collection has some these days. For instance, the subtle fabric I chose for the background of Full Bloom Quilt (page 80) I found in the baby section of fabrics of the quilt store. The rest of the collection was bright and busy, but this fabric was one that played well with other collections. Low volumes and blenders are truly my favorite kind of neutral as a print-fabric lover.

COLOR

Add color into the mix, and you have a whole other set of design decisions to make. Color is the cherry on top of the fabric choices. A good design is essential to any fabric; a great color is a bonus. For me, fabric selection starts with a pattern and color that make my heart jump—that special fabric that cries out to me, just begging me to use it. I think of it as the focal fabric. The right focal fabric gives you a place to build your whole color palette for a project. I select the rest of my fabrics to coordinate with, but not necessarily match, that initial focal print. Interestingly, that focal fabric may never make it into the final project, or it may be the backing for a project. But even so, it has provided inspiration.

A great palette for a quilt is anything that you love. That may seem like a cop-out on giving you instructions for selecting fabrics, but I truly believe that if you love a selection of fabrics, then you will love your finished project. Any mix of colors can work when you find the right focal print or quilt

Study a color wheel to help you gain an understanding of how colors relate to each other when planning your fabric color palette.

Adding neutrals to your quilt gives the eye somewhere to rest, like in Carnival Quilt (page 114).

design to pull them all together. That said, there are some points to take into consideration when selecting a complete set of fabrics for a project.

Study a color wheel to help you gain an understanding of how colors relate to each other. There are entire books written by experts on color theory, and I would do this topic an injustice by trying to summarize it in this book. However, I will touch here on a few of the most basic color schemes.

On the simplest level, there are three types of colors—primary (red, yellow, and blue), secondary (green, orange, and purple), and tertiary (colors such as blue-green or orange-yellow that are mixes of a primary and secondary color). To achieve color harmony, you can use a number of different color schemes. The simplest is the complementary color scheme—two colors, such as red and green, that are across from each other on the color wheel. I love complementary colors because of the high contrast they provide. Others include harmonizing schemes (two colors side-by-side on the wheel) and analogous schemes (three adjacent colors). Any number of color schemes can work for a quilt—even a whole rainbow.

More than likely, you naturally gravitate toward one type of color scheme and are not even aware of it. Taking a quick look at your work and fabric stash will probably clue you in to your favorite colors to quilt with. I personally am a total sucker for blues and pinks with pops of yellow. And while I love to wear the color green, I find that I rarely sew with it. And I definitely stay far away from brown. I've always wanted to be one of those cool people who calmly live in a world of tan and camel neutrals, but here I am instead with pink hair. You can admire one aesthetic without it being your natural go-to. You can challenge yourself to work with a color scheme that isn't your first choice or live your life in the shades that you love. There is truly a color for everyone.

Although color schemes provide great guidelines, try to keep your palette from being too coordinated. Color schemes are most interesting when there is a pop of a color that is a bit unexpected, like the dark gray flower petals in Flower Power Quilt (page 74). I know that I have a good selection of fabrics when there is a fabric that rubs me the wrong way! The best way to avoid the pitfalls of overly coordinated color schemes is to pull your fabric selections from a variety of designers' fabric lines.

Don't forget neutrals. They can help ease together any number of colors. I rarely make a project without a neutral somewhere in the quilt. I love color, so sometimes it can be hard to select a "noncolor" as one of the fabrics in my project. But they always help balance the dynamic colors that I choose first. A neutral fabric gives your eyes a place to rest in the dance of colors and patterns—an essential moment in any design. Neutrals can be as obvious as a white or cream, or a less obvious navy, soft blue, black, or gray. Any fabric that lets your eyes rest is a neutral in your palette.

A WORD ABOUT THREAD

When working with cotton fabrics, as I do, I most often piece with cotton thread that matches my fabric or a universal neutral 80-wt polyester thread that just disappears. I'll admit that I've been known to use whatever I have around that is the right color, or, out of laziness, even what is already in the machine. But do as I say and not as I do! As with

Eventually, you will curate your own, personal stash of wonderful fabrics to choose from.

all tools and supplies, it is worth getting the best quality thread that you can afford. You will put a lot of work into making a quilt, and you don't want to make the process harder on yourself by using thread that constantly breaks as you are sewing. (If that is happening, by the way, check your needle—it might be too dull!)

I piece with a stitch length on the smaller side—somewhere between 2.2 and 2.5mm on my machine settings. This eliminates the need for backstitching at either end of a seam. Cotton thread works well for this because it will cling to your fabric a little more, holding those ends close together, and fine weight thread tightly pierces your fabric.

When I am quilting the backing, batting, and quilt top, I am a bit looser with my thread choices. It all depends on what I want to accomplish with my quilting. Do I want clear, straight-line quilting? Then I will probably use a heavier-weight cotton thread. Do I want to do free-motion machine quilting with a lot of movement? Then most likely I choose a polyester thread. For decorative stitches that have a bit of shine, I almost always use a rayon thread. When hand stitching, as I do for my bindings, I tend to use whatever thread I have in a color I have that matches. I think it's a holdover from my garment sewing days.

Take all these suggestions with a grain of salt. There are a lot of different threads out there, and each machine seems to prefer a different kind. I have two domestic machines that I use constantly, and I get different results from each with the same thread. Experiment to find the thread that you prefer to have on hand and the weight you prefer for particular types of sewing.

STILL STRUGGLING TO SELECT FABRIC?

Determine what you love most about fabrics. Is it color? Is it small- or large-scale prints? Is it texture? Just start with these questions and build from here. You can begin to curate your own personal collection of fabrics from all over the world or more close to home. Add interest to your favorite fabrics by collecting from multiple fabric collections by the same designer or design house. Let people who work in quilt shops help you! If you love their store, then you love their taste. I promise that they would be thrilled to help you put together a bundle of fabric for a quilt. It's probably the favorite part of their job.

Don't be afraid to start with one fabric you just have to have and grow from there. For example, my Bright Ideas Wall Hanging (page 94) was designed around a yardage of a small black-and-white striped fabric that I bought while on vacation. I purchased a couple of yards of it, knowing that it was a perfect basic but not knowing how I would use it. You can see in the wall hanging that I only used a small rectangle of the striped fabric in one place. But the whole design started with that one simple basic. The scale and colors combined sparked my imagination in a way that told me I needed to make a quilt with pencils. That's the power of a single fabric.

FEARLESS CURVED PIECING

CUTTING CURVED PIECES

I cut curved pieces from fabric in one of two ways—using templates with a rotary cutter or using a die-cutting machine. The die-cutter can be a great time-saver if the dies match the size of my templates or you can decide to adjust the pattern to accommodate a different size block. Some, but not all, of my patterns are compatible with a die-cutter. Paper or acrylic templates can be used in every situation.

When cutting pieces, always place the straight edge either crosswise or lengthwise on the fabric's straight of grain. This results in a bias curved area, perfect for easing to the opposite curve.

TEMPLATES

The template patterns for the projects in this book can be found on pages 129–139. Many of the projects use the same size templates to make finished Drunkard's Path units that measure either 3½" × 3½" (9 × 9cm), 4" × 4" (10 × 10cm), or 7" × 7" (18 × 18cm). So, you can actually use one set to cut out multiple projects. (These match the Accuquilt dies.)

Use your favorite method to transfer the template patterns onto paper or template plastic. This lightweight plastic is available at most quilting stores and online. You can cut it with scissors, a rotary cutter, or a craft knife. It makes durable templates that you can use repeatedly. For a thicker template, I would suggest cutting and glueing together multiple layers of the same template plastic.

Purchased acrylic curve templates can be used as alternatives to the paper template patterns in this book. Given the infinite variety of quarter-circle curve measurements available, use discretion when choosing to use a premade acrylic template designed by someone else. One thing to look out for is the radius of the inner curve. Even if the overall block measures the same size, the size of the inner curve radius can be literally anything. You can most likely do an easy substitution if you are making one of my patterns with a more traditional layout (such as the pillow set, Medallion Baby Quilt, or Arabian Nights Quilt). But as soon as you move to any of my patterns with "modern curve" blocks, you start running into trouble. It is actually fairly simple these days to get your own set of acrylic templates made from paper templates such as the ones in this book. The internet is

Be sure your roatry blade is sharp when cutting fabric.

a valuable resource and there are companies who now offer custom acrylic templates for a reasonable price. Also, I have no personal experience with this, but for those with access to a 3D printer, it looks like that is also a great way to get some custom templates for a fraction of the cost (obviously having already invested in the 3D printer). I know that my local library has a 3D printer that can be used for a nominal cost, so look into resources like this as well. This is one of those times when we can appreciate the advances in technology.

DIE CUTTERS

You can neatly cut curved pieces from fabric using templates. But there is another way that's even easier. Die cutters that have burst onto the quilting scene give all our hands a break from laboriously cutting intricate and odd-shaped pieces. Cutting a large number of template-based blocks is quick work with the help of these ingenious little machines designed for home use.

Throughout this book, I make use of AccuQuilt's diecutters and Drunkard's Path dies. Die cutters operate on one basic concept. You place your fabric on a cutting pad over your chosen die, which has inlaid "blades" protected with foam (to keep your fingers safe) and cover it with a matching cutting mat. Then, you crank the handle of the machine, and the machine's roller provides even pressure to push the pad through and cut the fabric. You can cut multiple layers of fabric at once. Follow the manufacturer's instructions for your particular machine, and it will cut out your fabric shapes accurately every time. I personally have upgraded to a hands-free model where I simply need to gently nudge my die toward the machine, and it pulls it through and cuts it on its own. One of my favorite bonuses of using this die cutter is that the dies provide a center notch on each piece for easy matching.

After sewing hundreds of curves, I came up with a method that works every time.

HOW TO CUT

When using templates, I first cut strips of fabric to the desired width. Then I cut each strip into squares. Finally, I lay the appropriate template on each square and cut around it. Unless you are fussy-cutting fabric to spotlight a particular motif, you can cut multiple pieces at once using a template. (Be sure your rotary cutter blade is sharp!) I find that I can easily cut two or three layers of fabric around a template shape without distortion.

If you are using a die cutter, simply fold the cut strip neatly over the die back and forth multiple times, to get as many pieces as possible from one pass through the cutter. You may need to allow for extra fabric width and length if using a die cutter. The ease of using the machine comes at the sacrifice of a bit more fabric waste.

SEWING CURVES

After sewing hundreds of curves, I came up with a method that works every time.

In this section, I present my tried-and-true method for sewing curves, as well as some alternative methods.

MY METHOD

I tried a number of options before I landed on the method that works best for me when sewing curves. I wanted to sew the two pieces together quickly but most importantly, accurately. It did me no good to sew the curves at top speed and then end up getting out the seam ripper to correct mistakes because I wasn't able to be precise enough. Likewise, I didn't have the luxury of sewing at a snail's pace. I've sewed hundreds, perhaps thousands, of curves, so I'm pretty confident that you will like my method.

PIECING

1. Mark the center of each piece along the curved edge (both convex and concave). To do this, simply fold the piece in half and give it a quick press just at the curved edge **(fig. 1)**. Then use one—yes, just one—pin to pin the convex and concave pieces together at the center, right sides together **(fig. 2)**.

2. Sew the pieces together in two steps. First, align the two pieces together along one straight edge of each **(fig. 3)**, and sew from that edge to the pin at the center, easing the two pieces together **(fig. 4)**.

3. Stop, trim your threads, and then repeat from the opposite side **(fig. 5)**.

The trick is to ignore the fact that you are stitching a curve. Pretend it is a straight seam. Mind over matter can really help you sew a curve. And truly, when the diameter of the curve is large, you practically are sewing a straight line. Make sure that the section of the seam where the needle is piercing

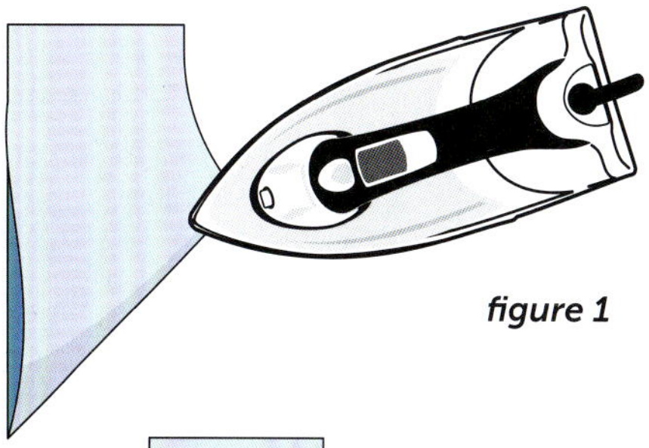

figure 1

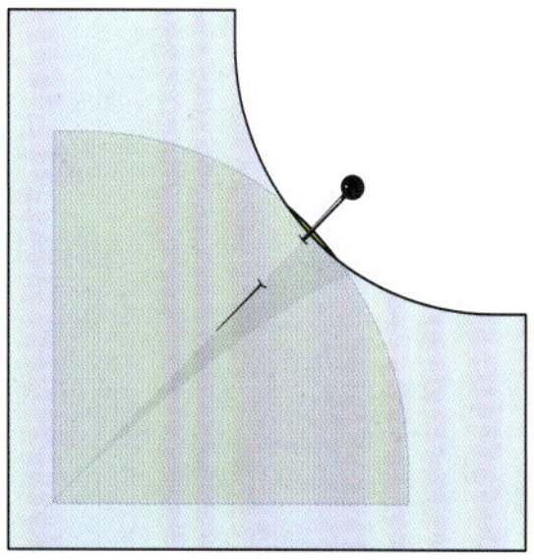

figure 2

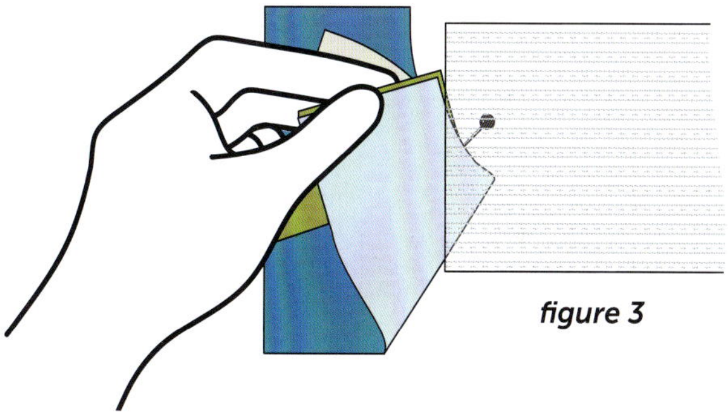

figure 3

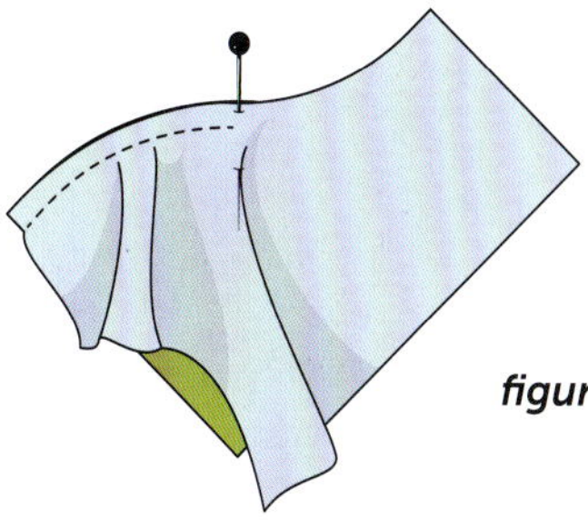

figure 4

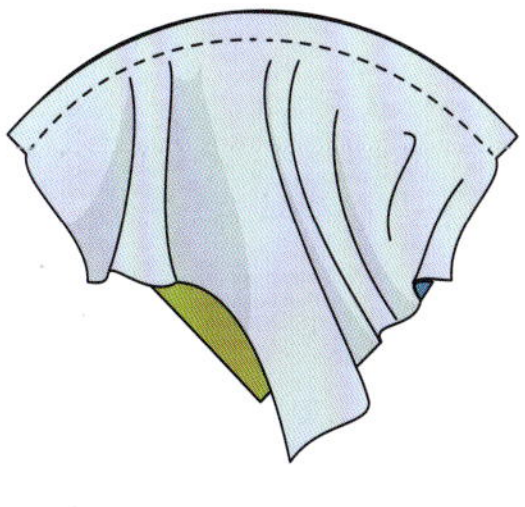

figure 5

the fabric always has the ¼" (6mm) seam allowance, and "forget" about the rest.

I find that this method gives me really clean ends to my quarter-circle curves, which is very helpful for the patterns that require precision. And I like sewing along the same outer curve the whole time. I can stay in one frame of mind while sewing. Plus, sewing to the middle each time gives me a chance to double check my first seam allowance when sewing the second half. No one is perfect, and sometimes a bit of re-sewing is necessary.

ALTERNATIVE METHODS

I know that we all see different ways to tackle the same job, and what works best for me may not be your favorite method. So, I'll mention some alternatives, and you can experiment with what method is best for you. Bottom line: Use the method that gets you the results you want. There is no one right way to sew these pieces together.

One popular method for sewing curved pieces together is to pin the pieces at multiple points along the entire curve, then sew continuously from one end to the other (Multiple-Pin Method). I put this in the category of always accurate, but slow. It's the method I started with when sewing curves, and it's a reliable way to do it.

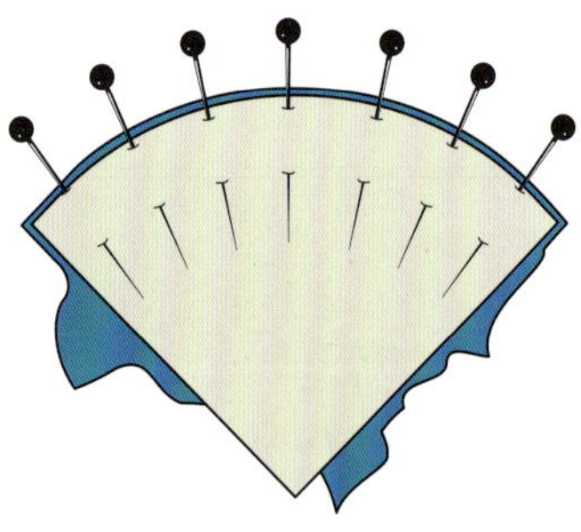

multiple-pin method

You might also try using just three pins—one at the middle and one on each end—and then sewing continuously from one end to the other (Three-Pin Method). I like this method for speed, and I find it fairly comparable to my method (although you don't get that chance to double check your seams). I have found it particularly useful when using this method to place your pins in such a way that you can easily sew over them.

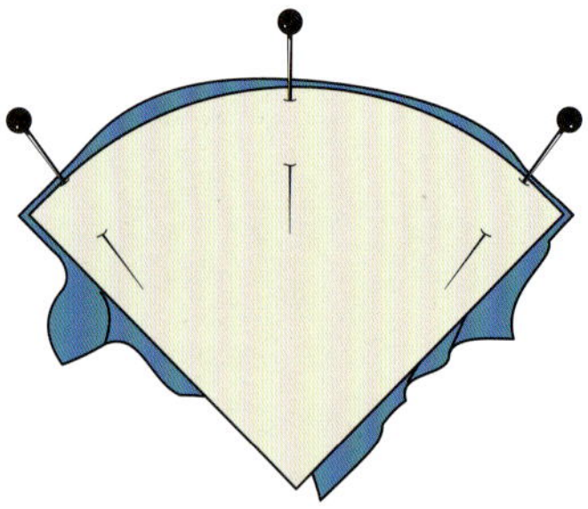

three-pin method

A lot of people swear by the No-Pin Method. They match up the two pieces and as they sew, they ease the fabric together with their hands along the entire seam from one end to the other. The No-Pin Method is a great method if you can do it. I personally find it difficult to get the ends to finish accurately, and I find it hard to evenly ease the fabric together without the help of the marked center.

Finally, another favorite method is also one that does not use pins (Glue Method), but instead of leaving the fabrics loose, they are carefully glued in place along the seam allowance. You can use a super-fine tip to glue baste with a bottle of liquid school glue or a small glue stick to hold the pieces together. Many will set the glue with a quick press of the iron to activate the glue. Just be sure to use a washable glue that will dissolve.

glue method

Having a wide variety of fabrics to choose from will come in handy when planning your project.

PRESSING

An important part of sewing curved pieces together is proper pressing. Contrary to popular belief, there is no need to clip the curves. The ¼" (6mm) seam allowance is slight and presses cleanly to either side of the seam.

I most often choose to press the seam allowance toward the inner curve because of the trimming and disappearing seams I use in many patterns throughout this book **(fig. 6)**.

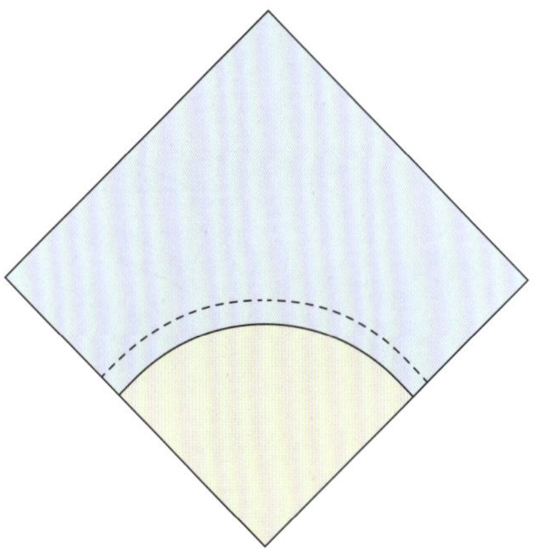

figure 6

1. Press the block first from the wrong side, gently pulling the smaller corner curve away from the seam. Press from the center and then on each end. As you press, do not put too much stress on this seam, because you can easily distort the square.

2. Flip the piece over and re-press the curve from the right side, double-checking that the fabric is pulled flat but not taut.

3. Finish up your quarter-circle block by trimming it with a rotary cutter as necessary. Curved blocks can easily get pulled out of square, so trimming is often necessary to square up the block. Using your ruler, square up your block to the desired size **(fig. 7)**.

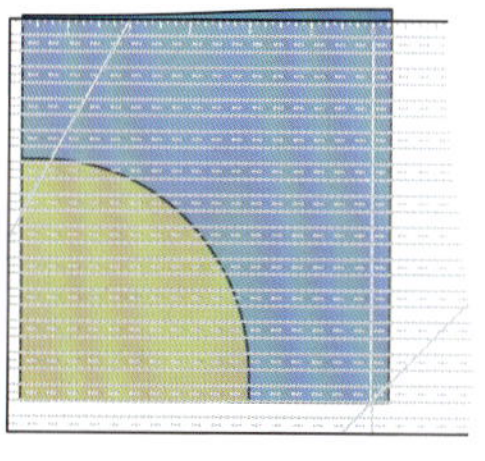

figure 7

MISTAKES HAPPEN!

Sewing curves quickly and simply is definitely doable, but some mishaps can occur. Here are three of the most common problems and the solutions for fixing them.

To prevent stretching in the first place, be gentler with your handling of the curved pieces. Since the curve on both pieces exposes the bias of the fabric, the pieces are vulnerable to stretching. This can happen when cutting, sewing, or pressing, or a combination of all three. Try to determine at what point in the process you are putting the most stress on the bias. Also note that some fabrics are more easily stretched than others, even though you are using the same technique to sew them. Some can make you feel like a rock star seamstress, and others make you want to throw in the towel.

PROBLEM #1

When sewing the curve, you end up with a tuck in your fabric. The fabric has bunched in one or more places and overlapped **(fig. 1)**.

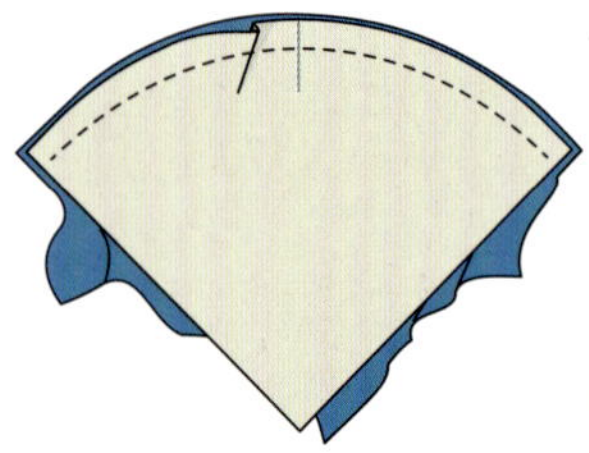

figure 1

SOLUTION

Make friends with your seam ripper. Tucks in the seam allowance of a curved piece are actually a very easy fix. Use your trusty seam ripper to rip out just a few small stitches over the offending tuck. Then take out one stitch on either side. Now you can easily stretch the fabric smooth **(fig. 2)**. Re-stitch the seam in place.

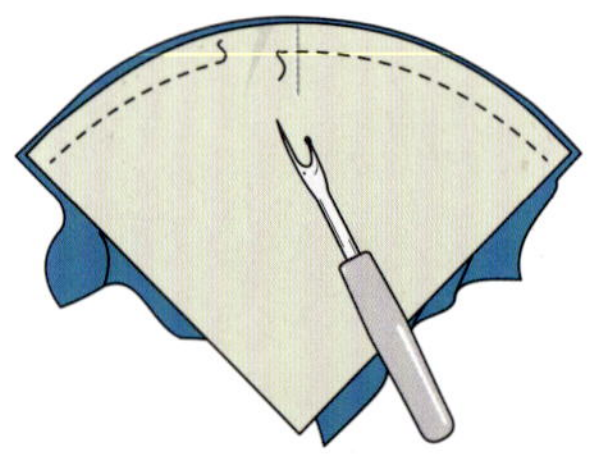

figure 2

PROBLEM #2

The ends of the curves do not align properly. One of them stretched, and the curve is uneven **(fig. 3)**.

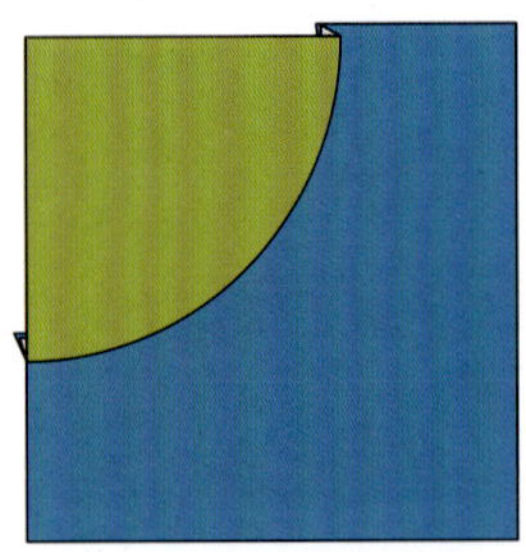

figure 3

SOLUTION

The fabric is not evenly eased throughout the curved seam. Seam ripper time again. Your best bet is ripping out the entire seam and starting again, carefully pinning the fabric together. Depending on where the ease went off, you might be able to partially rip the seam and resew it.

PROBLEM #3

Your finished block is obviously out of square **(fig. 4)**.

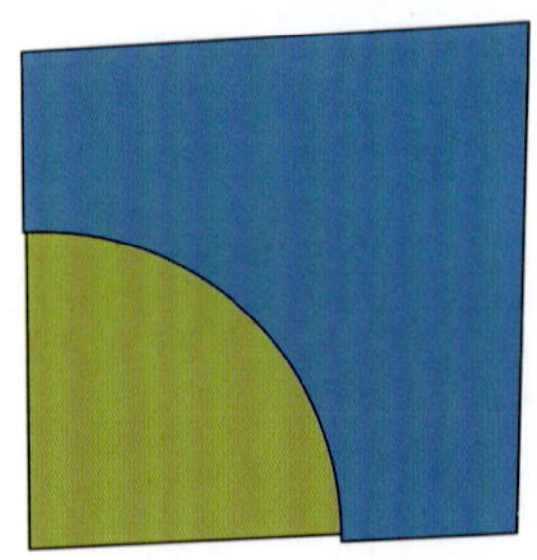

figure 4

SOLUTION

If it isn't too far off square, simply trim your block back into shape, as described in Step 3 of Pressing (page 17).

MODERN AND TRADITIONAL BLOCKS

There are two types of blocks you'll be using in this book—the "traditional," or classic, Drunkard's Path block, and what I call the "modern" Drunkard's Path block. The latter has a skinny leg on the L-shaped piece and a wider quarter-circle.

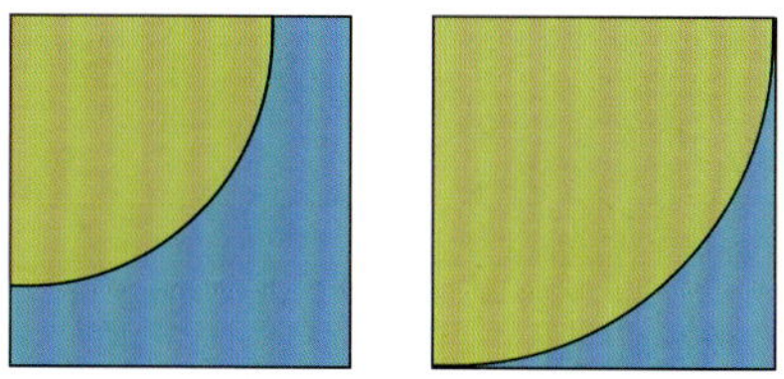

traditional block ***modern block***

To help make stitching easier when joining the modern-style A and B pieces, the L-shaped pieces are cut slightly oversized. (The quarter-circle portions are cut to size.) After sewing and pressing the curve, trim to the unfinished block size needed for the project. It's a little extra effort, but you'll find it's more accurate this way.

trimmed block

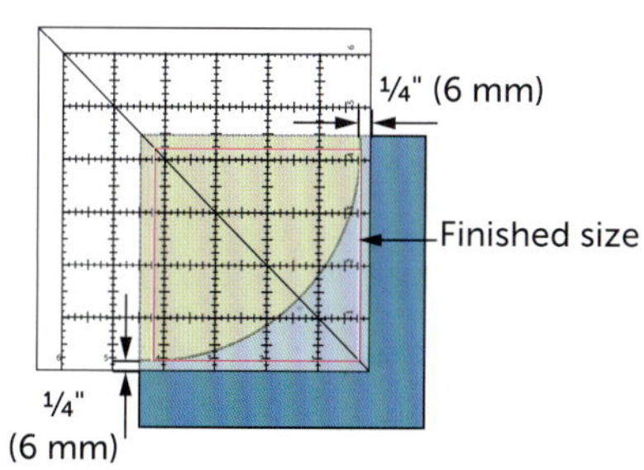

PUTTING BLOCKS TOGETHER

I use a technique that I call "disappearing seams" to join two modern Drunkard's Path blocks. Each modern Drunkard's Path block is trimmed down to a square with a 1/4" (6mm) seam allowance left on the L-shaped pieces' outer edges. When two of these blocks are sewn together, the outer 1/4" (6 mm) seams literally disappear. You are left with only the smooth curves meeting perfectly together at each end.

Correct pressing is essential to creating smooth, disappearing seams. You will need to press the seam allowance toward the inner curve. This reduces the bulk of sewing together two blocks with a 1/4" (6mm) seam allowance. If you pressed the seams toward the outer curve, then you would have six layers of fabric, rather than two, to sew through at the seam.

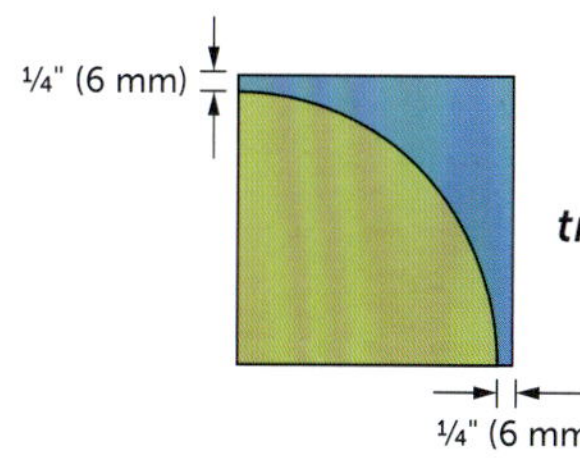

trimmed block

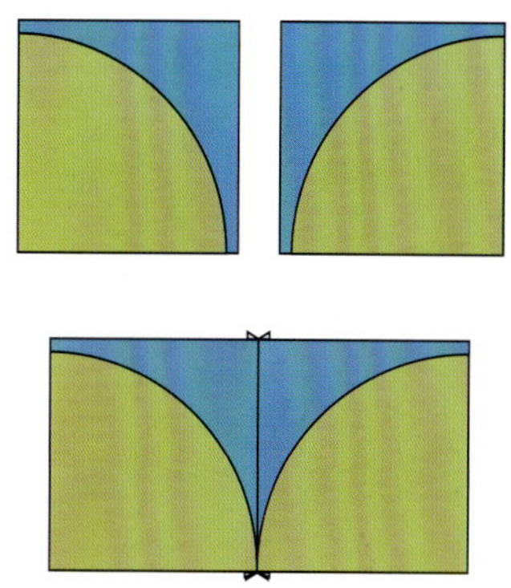

disappearing seams

PROJECTS

In this section are 16 projects that are based on Drunkard's Path blocks. Add a wealth of prints and solids, colors, blocks, and layouts, and make some wonderful quilted creations. Make a small coaster or a big, full-size quilt, a piece of wall art, or something for a new baby's crib. Follow the color schemes shown in the photos, or create something entirely new! Some of the projects share template patterns, while others have their own unique template patterns. Many use both shared and unique patterns. Each template pattern has a designated letter (A, B, C, and so on). Pay careful attention that you are using the correct ones for your chosen project. Template patterns are at the back of this book starting on page 129.

SIP AND STITCH COASTERS

Finished size: 5" (13cm) round circle
Designed, pieced, and quilted by Angela Pingel

Are curves completely new and completely scary to you? Then this is the perfect way to dive into a new versatile shape in sewing. The goal of making these coasters is to master using a template to cut out a curve and learn to sew along a circle edge with a ¼" seam allowance. You will notice that the coaster itself is round, so we are not even trying to square those circles off as we will do in every other project in the book. This is a low-stakes project with high reward. Go ahead and raid your scraps to make one, five, or 100 coasters. Embrace curves and get your skills ready to advance to the next level. Directions are for making a single coaster. Repeat to create as many as desired.

MATERIALS

4 squares 3" × 3" (8 × 8cm) of coordinating fabrics

1 square 6" × 6" (15 × 15cm) backing fabric

1 square 6" × 6" (15 × 15cm) batting

TOOLS

Template pattern B

Template plastic or paper

Tweezers and point maker (optional)

Hand sewing needle

CUTTING

- Cut 4 pieces B from the 3" × 3" (8 × 8cm) squares.
- Cut 1 square 6" × 6" (15 × 15cm) from the backing fabric.
- Cut 1 square 6" × 6" (15 × 15cm) from the batting.

TIP

This project is perfect for all your scraps of fabric and batting! You can also fussy cut a special fabric to achieve a coaster that is picture perfect.

MAKING THE COASTER

1. Begin by sewing the four quarter-circles together into two pairs along the 3" (7.6cm) edge in the orientation shown to create two half-circle pieces **(fig. 1)**. Press seams open.

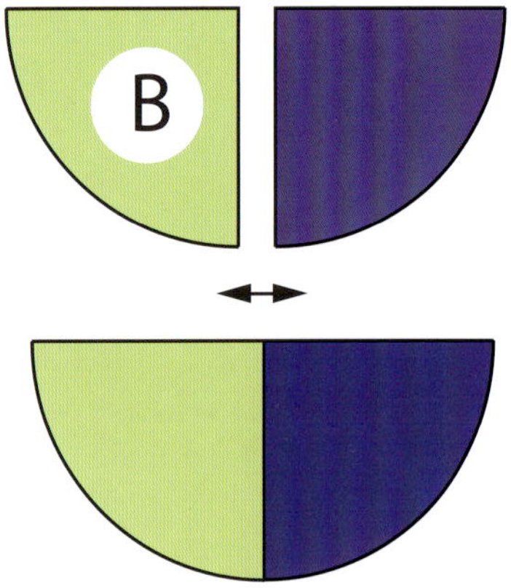

figure 1

2. Sew the two half-circle pieces together along the 5½" (14cm) edge to form a full circle matching center seam **(fig. 2)**. Press seams open.

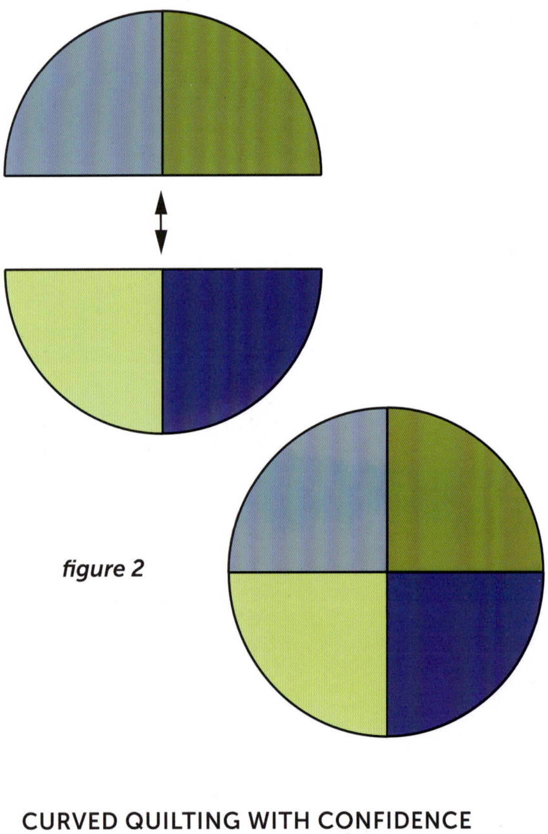

figure 2

3. Pin or baste your circle to your 6" × 6" (15 × 15cm) square of batting, wrong side together with the batting. Quilt as desired. I quilted my coasters with random overlapping lines to keep this project nice and simple, but another great idea is to quilt in concentric circles. Trim the batting to the circle edge.

4. Place the quilted circle right sides together with the 6" × 6" (15 × 15cm) square of backing fabric. Beginning at the end of one quarter-circle, stitch a ¼" (6mm) seam allowance from the edge of the circle. Stop stitching near the beginning of that same quarter-circle, leaving an unsewn gap of a few inches along the edge for turning **(fig. 3)**. Trim away excess backing fabric to leave just the circle.

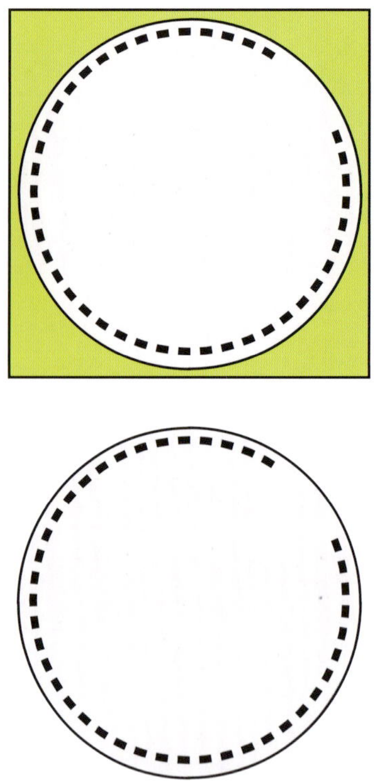

figure 3

5. Using the gap in the fabrics you left, turn the coaster right side out. You may find tweezers helpful to grip the fabric while flipping it right side out. Smooth out the inside edges of the circle with a small tool such as a point maker, chopstick, or butter knife.

6. Turn in the seam allowance in the open gap ¼" (6mm) on both sides and hand stitch the opening closed with a small slip stitch **(fig. 4)**.

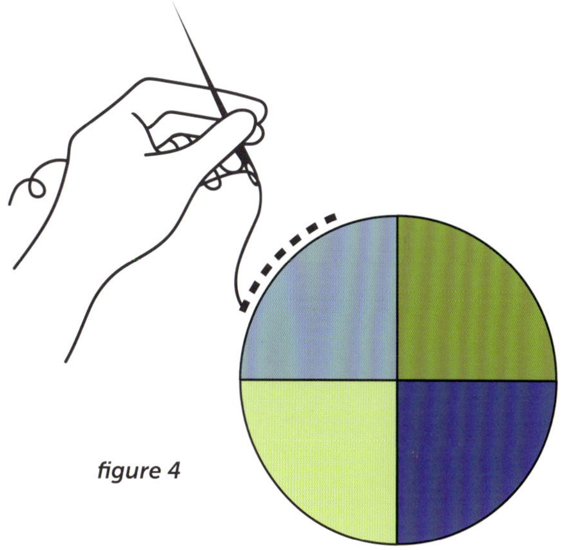

figure 4

PAIR OF PILLOWS

Pillow projects let you dip your toes into the water of curved piecing without getting soaked. Here are two classically based designs that use traditional Drunkard's Path layouts. As a pair, these pillows are striking when made in coordinating color schemes. Both pillows use the same number of units, but the result is amazingly different. The projects give you just a taste of the versatility of the quarter-circle unit and how it can be manipulated to yield a myriad of patterns. Both pillows are constructed the same way, with pieced and quilted tops, a full lining, zippered back, and binding. They give you an opportunity to try out many of the methods that you will use for larger projects, but on a much smaller scale. Remember, don't be afraid to change up the color schemes and make these patterns your own.

TEMPLE PILLOW

Finished size: 19½" × 19½" (49.5 × 49.5cm)
Designed, pieced, and quilted by Angela Pingel

Perhaps all you will ever want to make with curves is a pillow. This project size can be much easier to mentally handle versus a large quilt. Give this pillow a try when you are comfortable with the idea of curved piecing but just want a small project to tackle. Using only a few fabrics, the Temple Pillow pattern packs a lot of punch.

MATERIALS

Fabric amounts are based on yardage with a usable width of 42" (106.5cm).

½ yd (45.5cm) low-volume fabric

1 fat quarter pink print fabric

1 fat quarter gold print fabric

1 fat quarter dark blue print border fabric

1 yd (91.5cm) lining fabric

⅓ yd (30.5cm) backing fabric

3½" × 20" (9 × 51cm) fabric strip for zipper placket cover

¼ yd (23cm) binding fabric

20" (51cm) zipper

¼" (6mm) wide paper-backed fusible web tape

24" × 24" (61 × 61cm) batting

20" × 20" (51 × 51cm) pillow form

TOOLS

Template patterns A and B or 3½" (9cm) AccuQuilt die and cutter (page 14)

Template plastic or paper (if using patterns)

Zipper foot

CUTTING

WOF = width of fabric

FROM LOW-VOLUME FABRIC:

- Cut 2 strips 4½" (11.5cm) × WOF. Cut 13 pieces A from the strips.
- Cut 2 strips 4" (10cm) × WOF. Cut 12 pieces B from the strips.

FROM PINK PRINT FABRIC:

- Cut 3 strips 4½" × 22" (11.5 × 56cm). Cut 12 pieces A from the strips.

FROM GOLD PRINT FABRIC:

- Cut 4 strips 4" × 22" (10 × 56cm). Cut 13 pieces B from the strips.

FROM DARK BLUE PRINT BORDER FABRIC:

- Cut 4 strips 2" × 22" (5 × 56cm).

FROM LINING FABRIC:

- Cut 1 piece 20" × 20" (51 × 51cm) and 2 pieces 10½" × 20" (26.5 × 51cm).

continued on next page

FROM BACKING FABRIC:

- Cut 2 pieces 10½" x 20" (26.5 x 51cm).

FROM BINDING FABRIC:

- Cut 3 strips 2½" (6.5cm) x WOF.

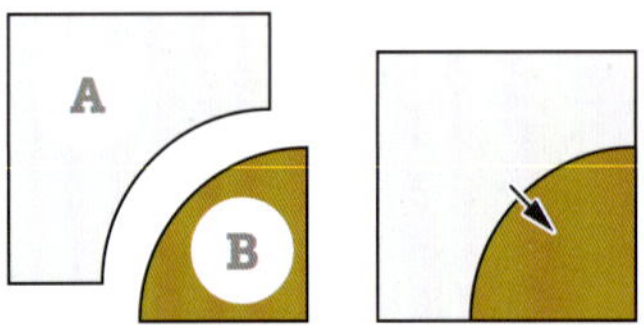

figure 1

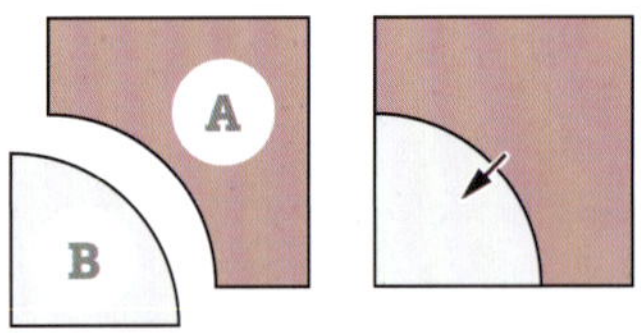

figure 2

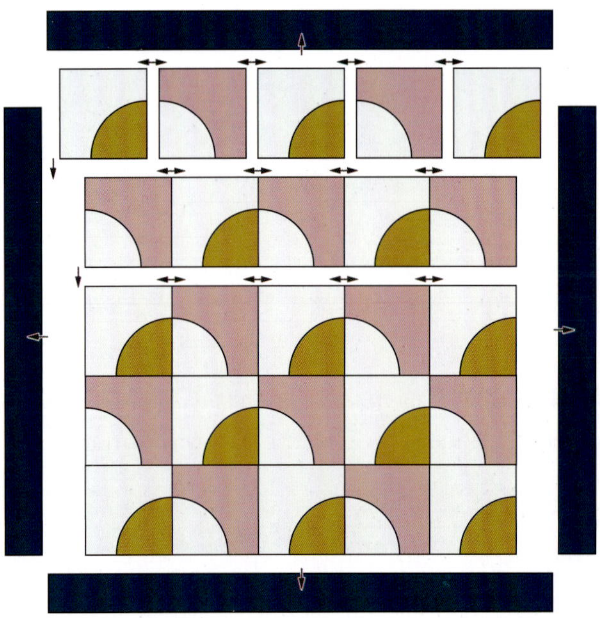

TEMPLE PILLOW CONSTRUCTION DIAGRAM

MAKING THE BLOCKS

Unfinished block size: 4" × 4" (10 × 10cm)
This pillow top has 25 blocks.

1. Sew each low-volume piece A to a gold print piece B **(fig. 1)**.

2. Sew each pink print piece A to a low-volume piece B **(fig. 2)**. Press all seams toward the B piece. You will have a total of 25 quarter-circle blocks. Trim the blocks to 4" × 4" (10 × 10cm) square.

MAKING THE PILLOW TOP

1. Arrange the blocks in five rows of five blocks each, as shown in the Temple Pillow Construction Diagram, alternating colors and block orientation as shown.

2. Sew the blocks together into rows, matching adjacent seams. Press the seams open.

3. Sew the rows together, matching adjacent seams. Press the seams in one direction.

4. Trim two of the border strips to 2" × 18" (5 × 45.5cm) and the other two to 2" × 21" (5 × 53.5cm). Sew the shorter strips to opposite sides of the pillow. Press the seams toward the border. Sew the longer strips to the remaining sides of the pillow. Press the seams toward the border.

5. Baste the pillow top to the batting. Using your favorite method, quilt as desired. I used simple stitch-in-the-ditch quilting to emphasize the curves of the blocks and let the fabric remain unobstructed. Trim the pillow top to 20" × 20" (51 × 51cm) square. To finish, see Constructing the Pillows on page 31.

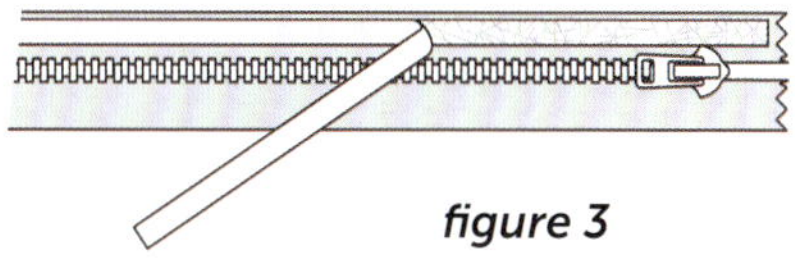

figure 3

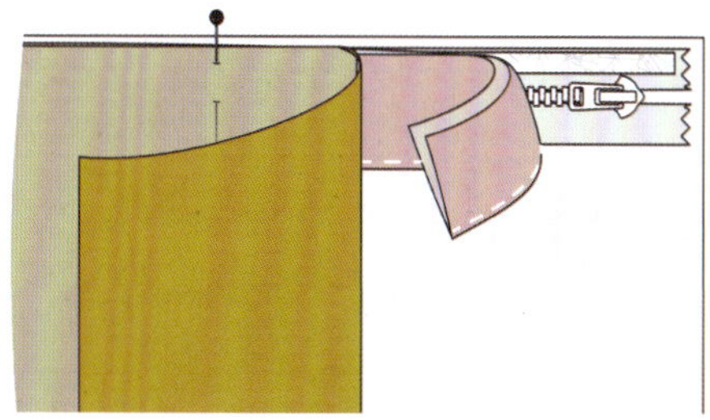

figure 5

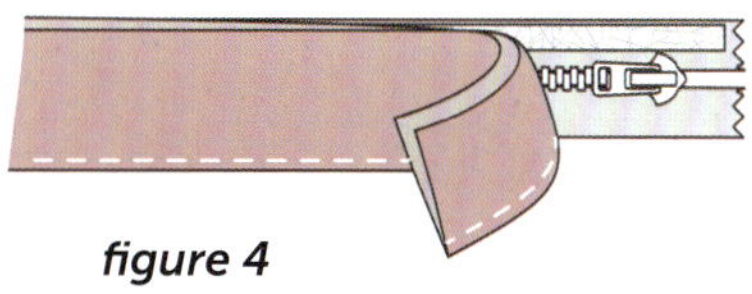

figure 4

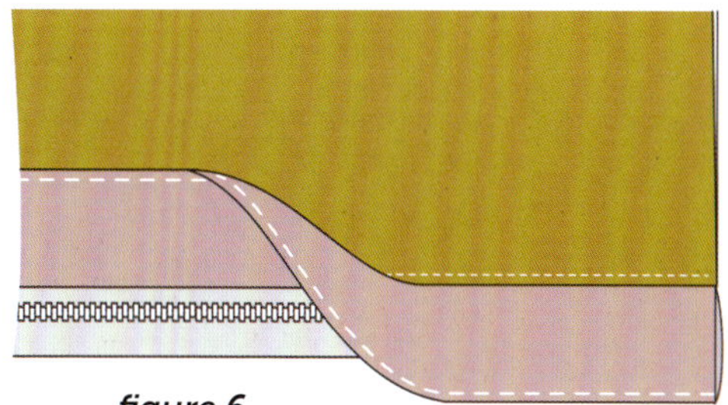

figure 6

CONSTRUCTING THE PILLOW

1. Baste the 20" x 20" (51 x 51cm) lining fabric to the batting side of the pillow top. Sew the fabric in place using a scant ¼" (6mm) seam around the perimeter of the pillow. Set the top aside.

2. Fold the zipper placket fabric in half lengthwise with wrong sides together, and press. Topstitch along the folded edge.

3. Following the manufacturer's directions, use your iron to fuse the paper-backed fusible web to one side of the zipper, along the length **(fig. 3)**.

4. Peel off the paper from the fusible, and fuse the folded zipper placket along the length of the zipper, matching the raw edges of the fabric to the upper long edge of the zipper **(fig. 4)**.

5. Place the layers of the pillow back together along the 20" (51cm) length as follows. Lay one of the 10½" x 20" (26.5 x 51cm) lining pieces right side up, the zipper teeth up (with placket attached), and one of the 10½" x 20" (26.5 x 51cm) backing pieces right side down **(fig. 5)**. Pin the layers together.

6. Attach a zipper foot to your sewing machine, and stitch along the zipper, moving the zipper pull as necessary. Fold the fabric and placket seam allowances away from the zipper and topstitch in place **(fig. 6)**.

7. Repeat steps 5 and 6 to complete the other side of the pillow back and lining. (Note that there is no placket in this step.)

8. Trim the pillow back, zipper, and lining to 20" x 20" (51 x 51 cm) square if necessary.

9. Layer the pillow back and pillow top, wrong sides together. Baste around the pillow perimeter.

10. Follow the steps described in Binding (page 126) to sew the binding strips together, and sew the binding to the perimeter of the pillow to finish all the edges.

11. Stuff your pillow with a square 20" x 20" (51 x 51cm) pillow form, and zip it closed.

BOW TIE PILLOW

Finished size: 19½" × 19½" (49.5 × 49.5cm)
Designed, pieced, and quilted by Angela Pingel

This sweet pillow is one of the simplest patterns in terms of curves in the entire book. Dive into curved piecing and get your feet wet with this project. With 25 small, curved blocks to sew, the pattern is both manageable and quick. The added bonus of this design is that there is no attempt to match curved seams together as I do with most patterns here. I would consider this the most traditional design I share in the book, and it proves just how strong the classic designs already are.

MATERIALS

Fabric amounts are based on yardage with a usable width of 42" (106.5cm).

⅝ yd (57cm) low-volume fabric

1 fat quarter blue print fabric

1 fat quarter gold print fabric

1 fat quarter dark blue print border fabric

1 yd (91.5cm) lining fabric

⅓ yd (30.5cm) backing fabric

3½" × 20" (9 × 51cm) fabric strip for zipper placket cover

¼ yd (23cm) binding fabric

20" (51cm) zipper

¼" (6mm) wide paper-backed fusible web tape

24" × 24" (61 × 61cm) batting

20" × 20" (51 × 51cm) pillow form

TOOLS

Template patterns A and B or 3½" (9cm) AccuQuilt die and cutter (page 14)

Template plastic or paper (if using patterns)

Zipper foot

CUTTING

WOF = width of fabric

FROM LOW VOLUME FABRIC

- Cut 4 strips 4½" (11.5cm) × WOF. Cut 25 pieces A from the strips.

FROM GOLD PRINT FABRIC

- Cut 3 strips 4" × 22" (11.5 × 56cm). Cut 13 pieces A from the strips.

FROM BLUE PRINT FABRIC

- Cut 3 strips 4" × 22" (10 × 56cm). Cut 12 pieces B from the strips.

FROM DARK BLUE PRINT BORDER FABRIC

- Cut 4 strips 2" × 22" (5 × 56cm)

FROM LINING FABRIC

- Cut 1 piece 20" × 20" (51 × 51cm) and 2 pieces 10½" × 20" (26.5 × 51cm).

FROM BACKING FABRIC

- Cut 2 pieces 10½" × 20" (26.5 × 51cm).

FROM BINDING FABRIC

- Cut 3 strips 2½" (6.5cm) × WOF.

MAKING THE BLOCKS

Unfinished block size: 4" x 4" (10 x 10cm)
This pillow top has 25 blocks.

1. Sew a low-volume piece A to each gold print piece B and blue print piece B **(fig. 1)**.

2. Press all seams toward the B piece. You will have a total of 25 quarter-circle blocks. Trim the blocks to 4" x 4" (10 x 10cm) square.

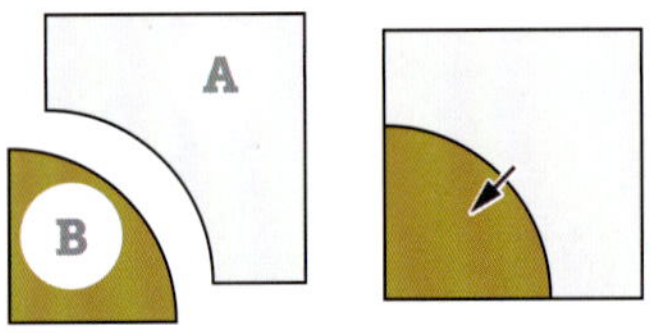

figure 1

BOW TIE PILLOW CONSTRUCTION DIAGRAM

MAKING THE PILLOW TOP

1. Arrange the blocks in five rows of five blocks each, as shown in the Bow Tie Pillow Construction Diagram, alternating colors and block orientation as shown.

2. Sew the blocks together into rows, matching adjacent seams. Press the seams open.

3. Sew the rows together, matching adjacent seams. Press the seams in one direction.

4. Trim two of the border strips to 2" x 18" (5 x 45.5cm) and the other two to 2" x 21" (5 x 53.5cm). Sew the shorter strips to opposite sides of the pillow. Press the seams toward the border. Sew the longer strips to the remaining sides of the pillow. Press the seams toward the border.

5. Baste the pillow top to the batting. Using your favorite method, quilt as desired. I quilted simple fan lines and hand stitched accents on the blue areas, outlines on the aqua curves, and left the white areas unquilted. Trim the pillow top to 20" x 20" (51 x 51cm) square.

6. Follow the instructions for Constructing the Pillows (page 31) to finish your pillow.

MEDALLION BABY QUILT

Finished size: 42" × 42" (106.5 × 106.5cm)
Designed, pieced, and quilted by Angela Pingel

This colorful and cheerful quilt is perfect for the newest baby in your life. The pattern translates well for either a boy or a girl, and the large blocks go together like a breeze. Consider making this quilt with a high-loft polyester batting and securely hand tying it to create a special, extra soft play mat for the baby. Think outside the box and try this with flannel or even cuddle fabrics for the ultimate snuggle factor.

SAFETY TIP

No buttons, please! They are hazardous if swallowed.

MATERIALS

Fabric amounts are based on yardage with a usable width of 42" (106.5cm), unless otherwise noted.

5/8 yd (57cm) yellow print fabric

5/8 yd (57cm) dark pink print fabric

1 yd (91.5cm) lavender print fabric

1 yd (91.5cm) dark blue print fabric

5/8 yd (57cm) red print fabric

1 1/2 yd (137cm) of 54" (137cm) wide home decorator-weight backing fabric (or 2 7/8 yd [2.7m] of 45" [114.5cm] wide fabric)

3/8 yd (34.3cm) binding fabric

50" × 50" (127 × 127cm) batting

TOOLS

Template patterns C and D or 7" (18cm) AccuQuilt die and cutter (page 14)

Template plastic or paper (if using patterns)

CUTTING

WOF = width of fabric

FROM YELLOW PRINT FABRIC:

- Cut 1 strip 9" (23cm) × WOF. Cut 4 pieces D from the strips.
- Cut 1 strip 10" (25.5cm) × WOF. Cut 4 pieces C from the strip.

FROM DARK PINK PRINT FABRIC:

- Cut 2 strips 10" (25.5cm) × WOF. From these strips, cut 4 pieces C and 8 pieces D.

FROM LAVENDER PRINT FABRIC:

- Cut 3 strips 10" (25.5cm) × WOF. From these strips, cut 8 pieces C and 12 pieces D.

FROM DARK BLUE PRINT FABRIC:

- Cut 3 strips 10" (25.5cm) × WOF. From these strips, cut 12 pieces C and 8 pieces D.

FROM RED PRINT FABRIC:

- Cut 2 strips 10" (25.5cm) × WOF. From these strips cut 8 pieces C and 4 pieces D.

continued on next page

FROM BACKING FABRIC:

- Cut 1 square 50" x 50" (127 x 127cm) from home decorator fabric, or 2 rectangles 50" (127cm) x WOF of 45" (114.5cm) wide fabric.

FROM BINDING FABRIC:

- Cut 5 strips 2½" (6.5cm) x WOF.

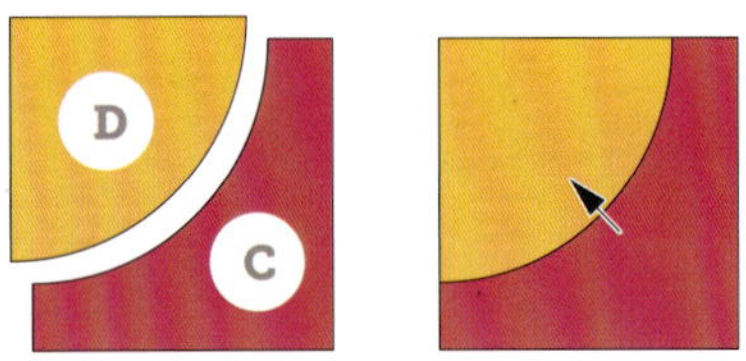

figure 1

MEDALLION BABY CONSTRUCTION DIAGRAM

MAKING THE BLOCKS

Unfinished block size: 7½" x 7½" (19 x 19cm)
This quilt has 36 blocks.

1. Sew together all the pieces C and D as follows **(fig.1)**:
   - Sew 4 yellow print pieces D to 4 dark pink print pieces C.
   - Sew 8 dark pink print pieces D to 8 lavender print pieces C.
   - Sew 12 lavender print pieces D to 12 dark blue print pieces C.
   - Sew 8 dark blue print pieces D to 8 red print pieces C.
   - Sew 4 red print pieces D to 4 yellow print pieces C.

   You will have a total of 36 quarter-circle blocks.
2. Press all seams toward the D piece. Trim the blocks to 7½" x 7½" (19 x 19cm) square.

MAKING THE QUILT TOP

1. Arrange the blocks into six rows of six blocks per row, as shown in the Medallion Baby Construction Diagram. Pay careful attention to the block orientation and color placement.
2. Sew the blocks together into rows, matching adjacent seams. Press the seams, alternating directions for each row.
3. Sew the rows together, matching adjacent seams. Press the seams in one direction.

FINISHING

1. Refer to Finishing Your Quilt (page 122) or use your favorite methods to layer and baste the quilt top, batting, and backing.

2. Quilt as desired. I quilted diagonal lines in a cross-hatch pattern through the corners of each block to contrast the pieced curves with the square stitching.

3. Bind your quilt using my French double-fold binding method as described in Binding (page 126) or your own preferred method.

TENNIS MATCH QUILT

Finished size: 67" × 90" (170 × 229cm)
Designed, pieced, and quilted by Angela Pingel

Put a spin on the classic Log Cabin design. The offset centers of the blocks give movement and interest to this quilt. A simple twist of one block is all it takes to create motion and send the ball bouncing in all directions. The result of mixing quarter-circle units using Log Cabin techniques is a pleasing balance of strips and curves that is a perfect match.

MATERIALS

Fabric amounts are based on yardage with a usable width of 42" (106.5cm).

1 fat quarter gray print fabric

1 fat quarter orange print fabric

1 fat quarter fuchsia print fabric

1 fat quarter blue print fabric

1½ yd (137cm) yellow stripe fabric

3⅛ yd (2.9m) medium green solid fabric

⅞ yd (80cm) light green print fabric

1⅜ yd (125.5cm) white solid fabric

2¼ yd (2m) charcoal solid fabric

5½ yd (5m) backing fabric

¾ yd (68.5cm) binding fabric

75" × 98" (191 × 250cm) batting

TOOLS

Template patterns A and B and/or 3½" (9cm) AccuQuilt die and cutter (page 14), and template patterns E and F

Template plastic or paper (if using patterns)

CUTTING

WOF = width of fabric

FROM GRAY PRINT FABRIC:

- Cut 3 strips 4" × 22" (10 × 56cm). Cut 12 pieces B from the strips.

FROM ORANGE PRINT FABRIC:

- Cut 3 strips 4" × 22" (10 × 56cm). Cut 12 pieces B from the strips.

FROM FUCHSIA PRINT FABRIC:

- Cut 3 strips 4" × 22" (10 × 56cm). Cut 12 pieces B from the strips.

FROM BLUE PRINT FABRIC:

- Cut 3 strips 4" × 22" (10 × 56cm). Cut 12 pieces B from the strips.

continued on next page

FROM YELLOW STRIPE FABRIC:

- Cut 19 strips 2½" (6.5cm) × WOF. From these, cut the following:
  - From 4 strips, cut 3 strips 2½" × 9½" (6.5 × 24cm) and 1 strip 2½" × 13½" (6.5 × 34.5cm) for a total of 12 strips 2½" × 9½" (6.5 × 24cm) and 4 strips 2½" × 13½" (6.5 × 34.5cm).
  - From 12 strips, cut 2 strips 2½" × 11½" (6.5 × 29cm) for a total of 24 strips and 1 strip 2½" × 9½" (6.5 × 24cm) for a total of 12 strips.
  - From the remaining 3 strips, cut 8 more strips 2½" × 13½" (6.5 × 34.5cm), for a total of 12.

FROM MEDIUM GREEN SOLID FABRIC:

- Cut 24 strips 4½" (11.5cm) × WOF. Cut 48 strips 4½" × 13½" (11.5 × 34.5cm) from the strips.

FROM LIGHT GREEN PRINT FABRIC:

- Cut 6 strips 4½" (11.5cm) × WOF. Cut 48 pieces F from the strips.

FROM WHITE SOLID FABRIC:

- Cut 6 strips 2½" (6.5cm) × WOF. Cut 12 strips 2½" × 9½" (6.5 × 24cm) and 12 strips 2½" × 7½" (6.5 × 19cm) from the strips.
- Cut 6 strips 5" (12.5cm) × WOF. Cut 48 pieces A from the strips.

FROM CHARCOAL SOLID FABRIC:

- Cut 7 strips 5½" (14cm) × WOF. Cut 48 pieces E from the strips.
- Cut 17 strips 2½" (6.5cm) × WOF. Cut 17 strips 2½" × 21½" (6.5 × 54.5cm) from the strips for sashing.
- From a 2½" (6.5cm) strip remnant, cut 6 squares 2½" × 2½" (6.5 × 6.5cm) for cornerstones.

FROM BACKING FABRIC:

- Cut 2 rectangles 98" (249cm) × WOF.

FROM BINDING FABRIC:

- Cut 9 strips 2½" (6.5cm) × WOF.

MAKING THE BLOCKS

Unfinished block size: 21½" × 21½" (53.5 × 53.5cm)
This quilt has 12 blocks.

1. Sew together the curved pieces A and B **(fig. 1)** as follows:
   - Sew 12 gray print B pieces to 12 white A pieces.
   - Sew 12 fuchsia print B pieces to 12 white A pieces.
   - Sew 12 orange print B pieces to 12 white A pieces.
   - Sew 12 blue print B pieces to 12 white A pieces.

   Press the seams toward the B pieces. You will have a total of 48 small quarter-circle units. Trim the units to 4" × 4" (10 × 10cm) square.

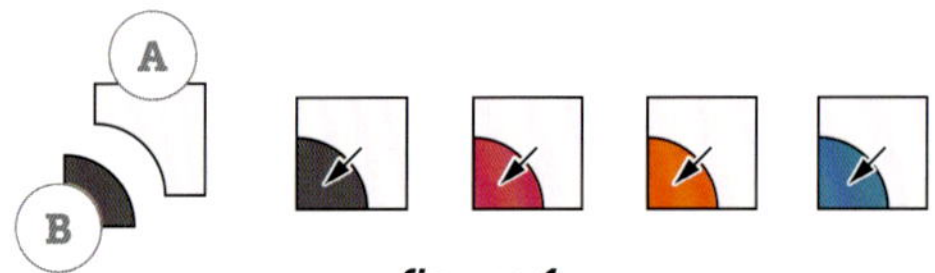

figure 1

2. Sew each blue/white unit to each orange/white unit matching adjacent seams. Press the seams open. Do the same with the fuchsia/white units and gray/white units **(fig. 2)**.

3. Sew the orange/blue units to the fuchsia/gray units, matching the adjacent seams to create the "tennis balls" **(fig. 2)**. Press the seams open, and trim the units to 7½" × 7½" (19 × 19cm) square. Make a total of 12 tennis ball units.

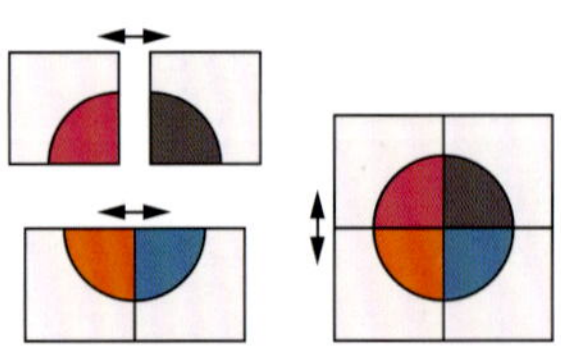

figure 2

4. With the "tennis ball" colors oriented as shown **(fig. 3)**, put together the Log Cabin style block as follows:
   - Sew a 2½" x 7½" (6.5 x 19cm) white strip to the right side of a tennis ball unit. Press the seam toward the white strip.
   - Sew a 2½" x 9½" (6.5 x 24cm) white strip to the top. Press the seam toward the white strip.
   - Sew a 2½" x 9½" (6.5 x 24cm) yellow stripe strip to the left side. Press the seam toward the yellow strip.
   - Sew a 2½" x 11½" (6.5 x 29cm) yellow stripe strip to the bottom. Press the seam toward the yellow strip.
   - Sew a 2½" x 11½" (6.5 x 29cm) yellow stripe strip to the right side. Press the seam toward the yellow strip.
   - Sew a 2½" x 13½" (6.5 x 34.5cm) yellow stripe strip to the top. Press the seam toward the yellow strip.

   Repeat to make a total of 12.

5. Sew a 4½" x 13½" (11.5 x 34.5cm) green solid strip to top and bottom of each Log Cabin block **(fig. 4)**. Press the seams toward the green strips.

6. Sew each charcoal solid piece E to each green print piece F **(fig. 5)**. Press the seams toward piece F. Trim the unit to 4½" x 4½" (11.5 x 11.5cm), leaving a ¼" (6mm) seam allowance on piece E.

7. Sew a green/charcoal unit to each end of the remaining 24 green solid strips 4½" x 13½" (11.5 x 34.5cm) **(fig. 6)**. Press the seams toward the green strips.

8. Sew these strips to the sides of each Log Cabin block, aligning adjacent seams, to complete 12 blocks **(fig. 7)**. Press the seams toward the green strip.

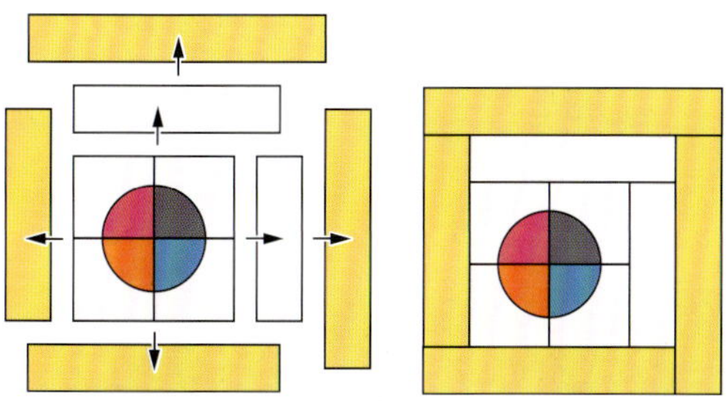

figure 3

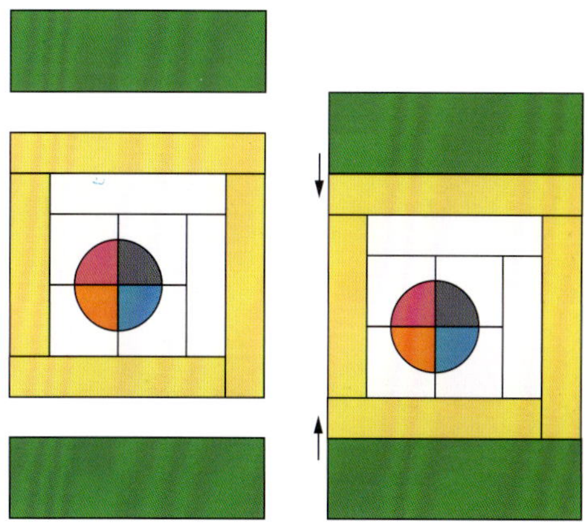

figure 4

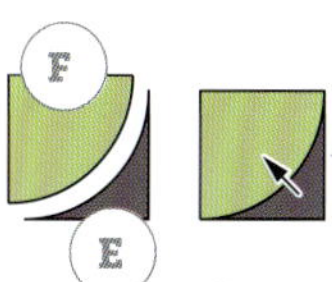

figure 5

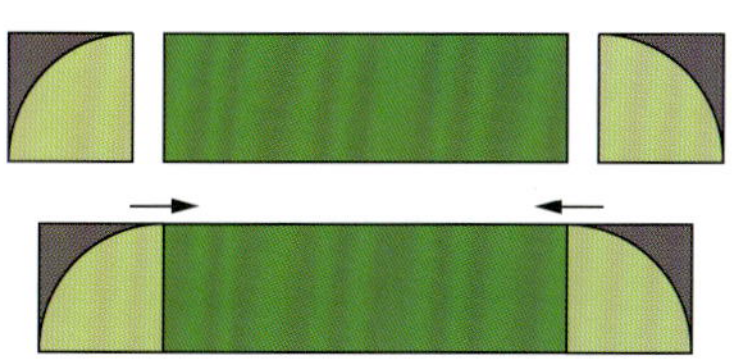

figure 6

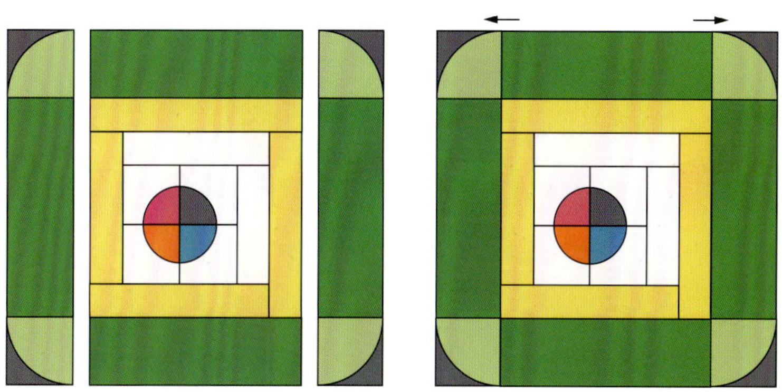

figure 7

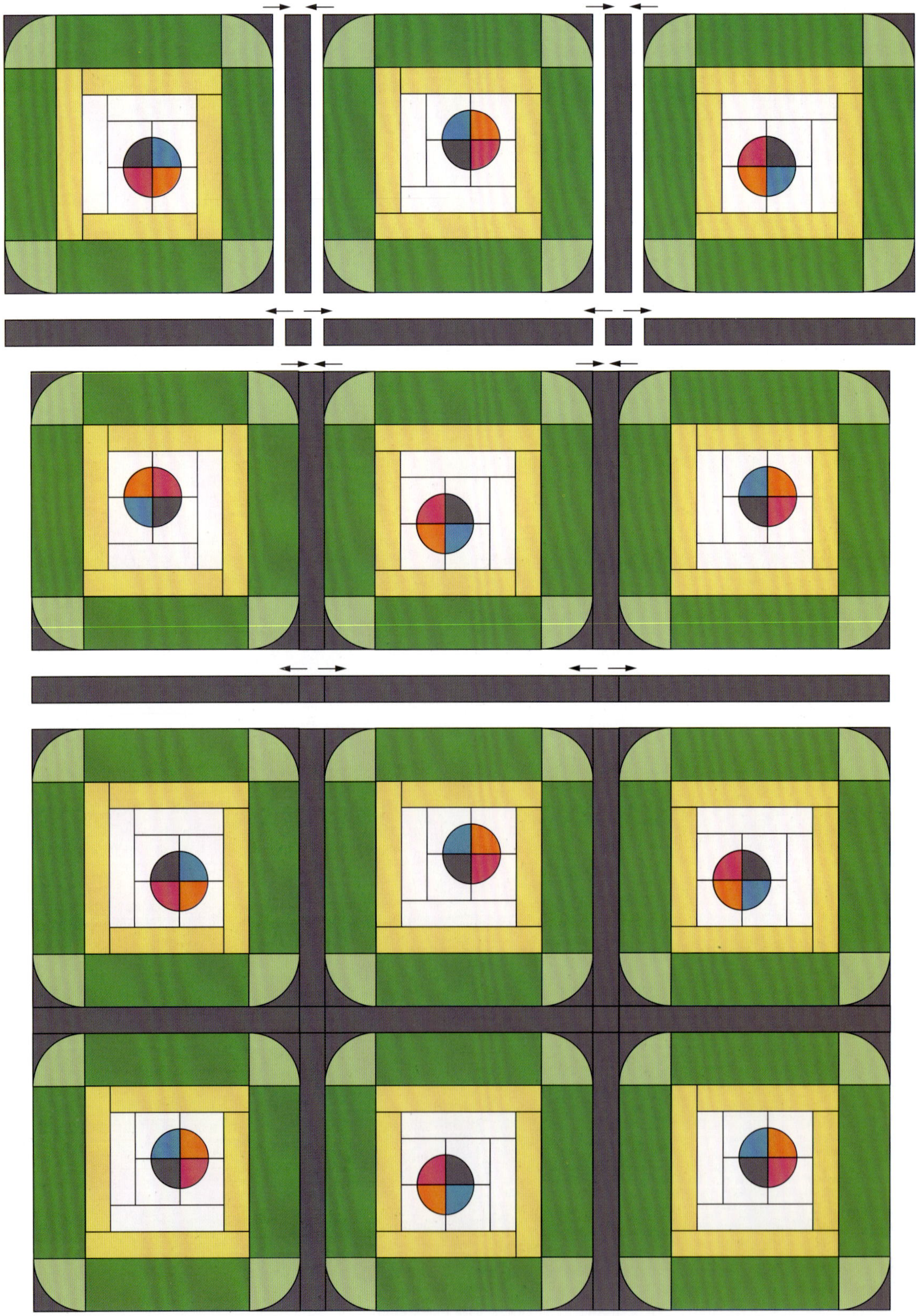

TENNIS MATCH CONSTRUCTION DIAGRAM

MAKING THE QUILT TOP

1. Arrange the blocks into four rows of three blocks each, as shown in the Tennis Match Construction Diagram, turning the blocks to create the "bouncing ball" effect. For each row, sew a charcoal sashing strip between the blocks. Press the seams toward the charcoal strip.

2. Sew the two charcoal cornerstone squares between three charcoal sashing strips to make three horizontal sashing rows.

3. Sew the block rows and sashings together to complete the quilt top, aligning all adjacent seams.

FINISHING

1. Refer to Finishing Your Quilt (page 122) or use your favorite methods to layer and baste the quilt top, batting, and backing.

2. Quilt as desired. I quilted wavy, vertical lines all across the quilt top.

3. Bind your quilt using my French double-fold binding method as described in Binding (page 126) or your own preferred method.

ARABIAN NIGHTS QUILT

Finished size: 56" × 72" (142 × 183cm)
Designed, pieced, and quilted by Angela Pingel

Arabian nights are calling, and the pull is strong. This traditional pattern is spiced up with 144 unique charm squares. With 12 large, tiled blocks, this is a perfect choice for a quilting bee. I pieced this quilt from Anna Maria Horner fabrics, as an homage to the beauty and cohesiveness of her many different fabric lines. Using a die-cutter helped make quick work of cutting the many pieces for this quilt.

MATERIALS

Fabric amounts are based on yardage with a usable width of 42" (106.5cm). Charm squares are 5" × 5" (12.5 × 12.5cm).

2⅝ yd (2.4m) white solid fabric

⅔ yd (61cm) navy print fabric

144 assorted charm squares

1⅞ yd (1.7m) orange print fabric for the borders

3⅝ yd (3.3m) backing fabric

⅝ yd (57cm) binding fabric

64" × 80" (162.5 × 203cm) batting

TOOLS

Template patterns G and H

Template plastic or paper (if using patterns)

CUTTING

WOF = width of fabric; LOF = length of fabric

FROM WHITE SOLID FABRIC:

- Cut 18 strips 5" (12.5cm) × WOF. From these, cut the following:
  - From 8 strips, cut 96 pieces G.
  - From 10 strips, cut 96 pieces H.

FROM NAVY PRINT FABRIC:

- Cut 4 strips 5" (12.5cm) × WOF. Cut 48 pieces G from the strips.

FROM CHARM SQUARES:

- Cut 48 pieces G.
- Cut 96 pieces H.

FROM ORANGE PRINT FABRIC:

- Cut a rectangle 64½" (164cm) × WOF. Cut 2 strips 4½" x 56½" (11.5 x 143.5cm) and 2 strips 4½" × 64½" (11.5 × 164cm).

FROM BACKING FABRIC:

- Cut 2 rectangles 64" (162.5cm) × WOF.

FROM BINDING FABRIC:

- Cut 7 strips 2½" (6.5cm) × WOF.

TIP

When assembling your blocks, try alternating warm and cool colors for a thoroughly balanced look to your quilt.

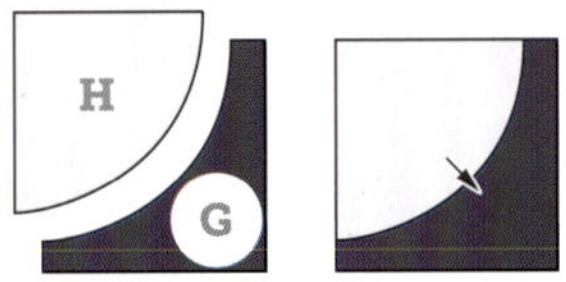

figure 1

figure 2

MAKING THE BLOCKS

Unfinished block size: 16½" x 16½" (42 x 42cm)
This quilt has 12 large, tiled blocks, each composed of 16 small blocks.

1. Sew together all the pieces G and H as follows **(fig. 1)**:
   - Sew 48 navy print pieces G to 48 white solid pieces H. Press the seams toward piece H.
   - Sew 48 charm square pieces G to 48 white solid pieces H. Press the seams toward piece G.
   - Sew 96 white solid pieces G to 96 charm square pieces H. Press the seams toward piece G.

   You will have a total of 192 quarter-circle units 4½" x 4½" (11.5 x 11.5cm).

2. Assemble the 12 large, tiled blocks using the units from Step 1. Each block is made up of 16 small units: four navy/white units, four charm/white units, and eight white/charm units. Orient the pieces as shown **(fig.2)**, and sew the blocks together. Press all seams open.

MAKING THE QUILT TOP

1. Refer to the Arabian Nights Construction Diagram to lay out the quilt top center in four rows of three large tiled blocks each. Sew together each row, aligning adjacent seams; press all seams open. Sew together the four rows to complete the quilt top center. Press all seams in one direction.

2. Sew the orange print borders to the quilt. Sew a strip 4½" x 64½" (11.5 x 164cm) to each side of the quilt. Press the seams toward the border. Sew a strip 4½" x 56½" (11.5 x 143.5cm) to the quilt top and bottom. Press the seams toward the border.

ARABIAN NIGHTS CONSTRUCTION DIAGRAM

FINISHING

1. Refer to Finishing Your Quilt (page 122) or use your favorite methods to layer and baste the quilt top, batting, and backing.

2. Quilt as desired. I quilted a simple crosshatch pattern over the whole quilt top.

3. Bind your quilt using my French double-fold binding method as described in Binding (page 126) or your own preferred method.

> **TIP**
>
> Don't have enough charms? Look online for charm swaps, or start one of your own! That's how I accumulated all my charms for this quilt.

PAINT DRIP QUILT

Finished size: 84" x 94" (213 x 239cm)
Designed and pieced by Angela Pingel
Quilted By Melissa Snyder of Longarm Louise

Can't you just feel the paint slipping down the walls with this design? This quilt would also be beautiful in monochromatic tones—perhaps blues to represent water droplets. Picture this quilt on a teenager's bed, and you will see one very happy teenager! (And who doesn't want that?) Long strips of high-contrast fabrics are very effective against a neutral print background. The starry prints read as solids from a distance, creating texture. For some extra fun, you can match your binding to the bottom paint splatters to create the illusion of paint slipping right off the quilt.

MATERIALS

Note: Fabric amounts are based on yardage with a usable width of 42" (106.5cm). Fabric amounts are also based on non-pieced long strips. This will yield a generous amount of extra fabric to use in another project.

¾ yd (68.5cm) lime green print fabric

1⅛ yd (102cm) yellow print fabric

1¾ yd (1.6m) pink print fabric

2⅛ yd (1.9m) rust print fabric

1¼ yd (114.5cm) light blue print fabric

1½ yd (137cm) bright blue print fabric

4¼ yd (4m) low volume print fabric

7¾ yd (7m) backing fabric

¾ yd (68.5cm) binding fabric

92" x 102" (234 x 259cm) batting

TOOLS

Template patterns G, H, J, and K

Template plastic or paper

CUTTING:

WOF = width of fabric;
LOF = length of fabric

All pieces are cut LOF, unless otherwise specified. Remember, if you find it easier, cut fabric squares before cutting out the Drunkard's Path pieces.

FROM LIME GREEN PRINT FABRIC:

- Cut 1 strip 6½" x 24" (16.5 x 61cm).
- Cut 6 squares 3½" x 3½" (8.9 x 8.9cm).
  - Subcut 6 pieces H.

FROM YELLOW PRINT FABRIC:

- Cut 1 strip 6½" x 35½" (16.5 x 90cm).
- Cut 1 strip 6½" x 15" (16.5 x 38cm).
- Cut 1 strip 9½" x 38½" (24 x 96.5cm).
- Cut 8 squares 3½" x 3½" (8.9 x 8.9cm).
  - Subcut 8 pieces H.
- Cut 2 squares 4½" x 4½" (11.4 x 11.4cm).
  - Subcut 2 pieces G.
- Cut 6 squares 5" x 5" (12.7 x 12.7cm).
  - Subcut 6 pieces K.

continued on next page

FROM PINK PRINT FABRIC:

- Cut 1 strip 6½" × 60" (16.5 × 152.5cm).
- Cut 1 strip 6½" × 26½" (16.5 × 67.5cm).
- Cut 1 strip 9½" × 29½" (24 × 75cm).
- Cut 1 strip 3½" × 18" (9 × 45.5cm).
- Cut 6 squares 3½" × 3½" (8.9 × 8.9cm).
  - Subcut 6 pieces H.
- Cut 4 squares 4½" × 4½" (11.4 × 11.4cm).
  - Subcut 4 pieces G.
- Cut 8 squares 5" × 5" (12.7 × 12.7cm).
  - Subcut 8 pieces K.

FROM RUST PRINT FABRIC:

- Cut 1 strip 6½" × 73½" (16.5 × 186.7cm).
- Cut 2 squares 3½" × 3½" (8.9 × 8.9cm).
  - Subcut 2 pieces H.

FROM LIGHT BLUE PRINT FABRIC:

- Cut 1 strip 9½" × 40½" (24 × 103cm).
- Cut 2 squares 5" × 5" (12.7 × 12.7cm).
  - Subcut 2 pieces K.
- Cut 4 squares 3½" × 3½" (8.9 × 8.9cm).
  - Subcut 4 pieces H.

FROM BRIGHT BLUE PRINT FABRIC:

- Cut 1 strip 9½" × 26½" (24 × 67.5cm).
- Cut 1 strip 6½" × 15" (16.5 × 38cm).
- Cut 1 strip 6½" × 50" (16.5 × 127cm).
- Cut 6 squares 5" × 5" (12.7 × 12.7cm).
  - Subcut 6 pieces K.
- Cut 2 squares 4½" × 4½" (11.4 × 11.4cm).
  - Subcut 2 pieces G.
- Cut 10 squares 3½" × 3½" (8.9 × 8.9cm).
  - Subcut 10 pieces H.

FROM LOW-VOLUME PRINT FABRIC:

Cut longest strips first, followed by shorter strips, and finish with pieces G, H, and J to minimize fabric waste. To minimize fabric waste, use the Background Fabric Cutting Diagram.

COLUMN 1:

- Cut 1 strip 6½" × 19" (16.5 × 48.5cm).
- Cut 1 strip 6½" × 41½" (16.5 × 105.4cm).

COLUMN 2:

- Cut 1 strip 6½" × 53½" (16.5 × 136cm).

COLUMN 3:

- Cut 1 strip 6½" × 77" (16.5 × 196cm).

COLUMN 4:

- Cut 1 strip 9½" × 3" (24 × 8cm).
- Cut 1 strip 9½" × 13½" (24 × 34.5cm).
- Cut 1 strip 9½" × 21½" (24 × 55cm).
- Cut 2 strips 2¼" × 6½" (6 × 16.5cm).

COLUMN 5:

- Cut 1 strip 6½" × 14" (16.5 × 36cm).
- Cut 1 strip 6½" × 12½" (16.5 × 32cm).

COLUMN 6:

- Cut 1 strip 6½" × 65½" (16.5 × 166cm).

COLUMN 7:

- Cut 1 strip 6½" × 15" (16.5 × 38cm).
- Cut 1 strip 9½" × 2" (24 × 5cm).
- Cut 1 strip 9½" × 28½" (24 × 72.5cm).

COLUMN 8:

- Cut 1 strip 6½" × 18½" (16.5 × 47cm.)

COLUMN 9:

- Cut 1 strip 9½" × 3" (24 × 8cm).
- Cut 1 strip 9½" × 41½" (24 × 105.5cm).
- Cut 2 strips 2¼" × 6½" (6 × 16.5cm).

COLUMN 10:

- Cut 1 strip 9½" × 9½" (24 × 24.2cm).
- Cut 1 strip 9½" × 27" (24 × 69cm).
- Cut 1 strip 9½" × 13½" (24 × 34.5cm).
- Cut 2 strips 2¼" × 6½" (6 × 16.5cm).

COLUMN 11:

- Cut 1 strip 6½" × 77" (16.5 × 196cm).

COLUMN 12:

- Cut 1 strip 6½" × 9½" (16.5 × 24.2cm).
- Cut 1 strip 6½" × 27" (16.5 × 69cm).
- Cut 5 strips 4½" (11.4cm) × WOF.
  - Subcut 36 squares 4½" × 4½" (11.4 × 11.4cm).
  - Subcut 36 pieces G.
- Cut 1 strip 3½" (8.9cm) × WOF.
  - Subcut 8 squares 3½" × 3½" (8.9 × 8.9cm).
  - Subcut 8 pieces H.
- Cut 4 strips 6" (15.2cm) × WOF.
  - Subcut 22 6" × 6" (15.2 × 15.2cm).
  - Subcut 22 pieces J.

FROM BINDING FABRIC:

- Cut 9 strips 2¼" × WOF.

FROM BACKING FABRIC:

- Cut 3 rectangles 92" (234cm) × WOF.

TIP

To keep the pieces organized, mark each piece with a scrap of paper indicating its size and pin in place. You will be forever thankful to have these measurements for assembly.

TIP

When cutting long lengths of fabric, roughly over-measure and cut a snip at the edge of the fabric. Rip the fabric at the snip, and press the ripped edge flat. Then rotary cut to size. Because you have over-measured your yardage, you will be able to cut away any of the area where the fabric's weave may have been distorted by ripping.

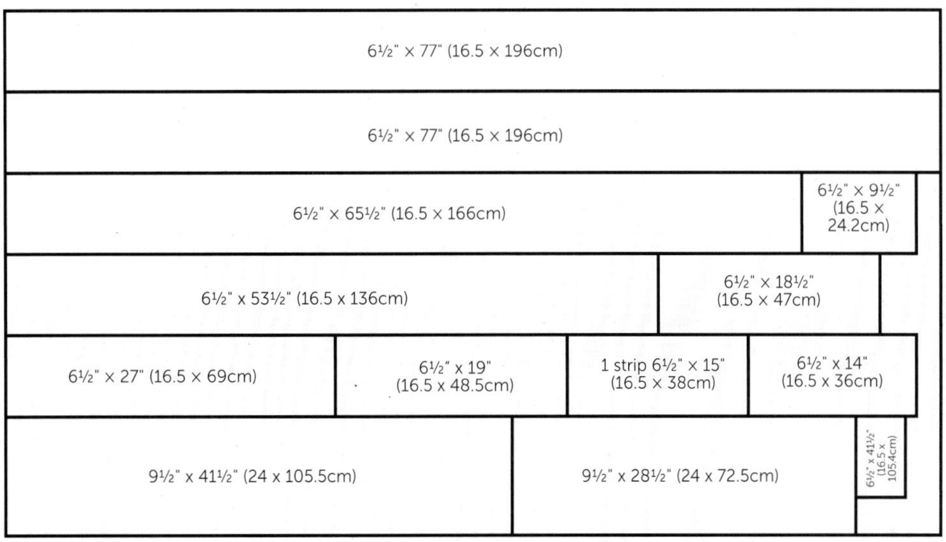

77" piece

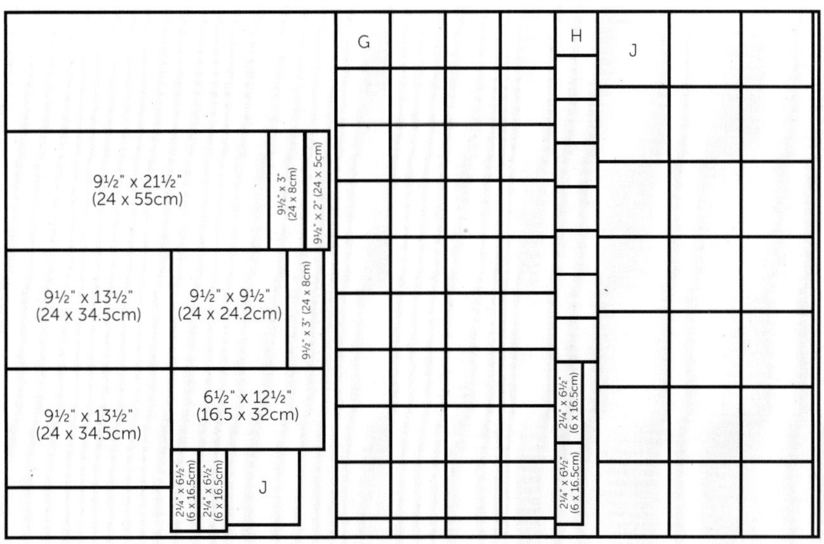

67" piece

BACKGROUND FABRIC CUTTING DIAGRAM

MAKING THE QUILT TOP

This quilt is assembled in 12 columns, which are then sewn together to complete the quilt top.

QUARTER-CIRCLE UNITS

Begin by making the quarter-circle units for all the columns.

1. Sew together the small curved pieces G and H as follows.
   - Sew 36 low-volume print pieces G to every color print pieces H. Press the seams toward piece H. Trim each unit to 3½" x 3½" (9 x 9cm) leaving a ¼" (6mm) seam allowance on the G piece **(fig. 1)**. You will have a total of 36 quarter-circle GH units. Arrange them into pairs by color.
   - Sew 8 low volume print pieces H to every color print pieces G. Press the seams toward piece H. Trim each unit to 3½" x 3½" (9 x 9cm) leaving a ¼" (6mm) seam allowance on the G piece **(fig. 2)**. You will have a total of 8 quarter-circle GH units with 2 yellow, 4 pink, and 2 bright blue G. Arrange them into pairs by color.
2. Sew the units from Step 1 into pairs to make nine half-circle units **(fig. 3)**. Press all seams open.
3. Sew 22 low-volume print pieces J to every color print pieces P. Press the seams toward piece K. Trim each unit to 5" x 5" (12.5 x 12.5cm) leaving a ¼" (6mm) seam allowance on the J pieces **(fig. 4)**. You will have a total of 22 quarter circles JK units with 6 yellow, 8 pink, 2 light blue, and 6 bright blue K.
4. Sew the units from Step 3 into matching pairs to make 11 half-circle blocks **(fig. 5)**. Press all seams open.

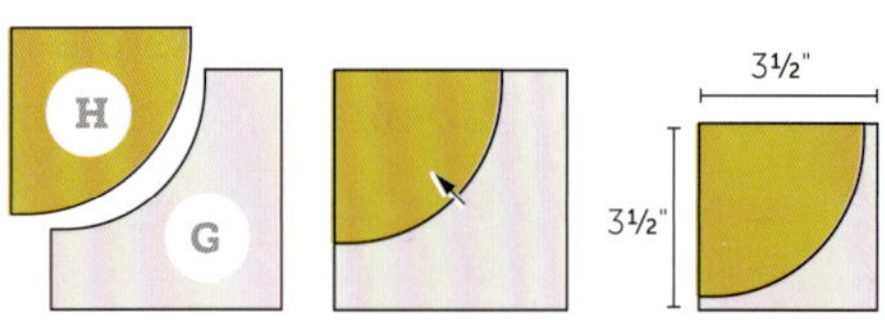

figure 1

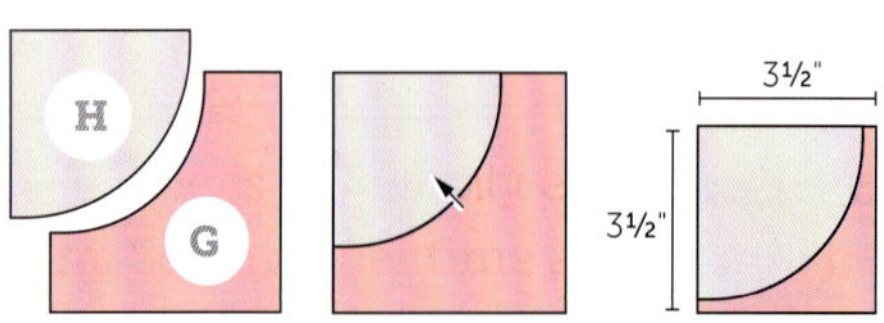

figure 2

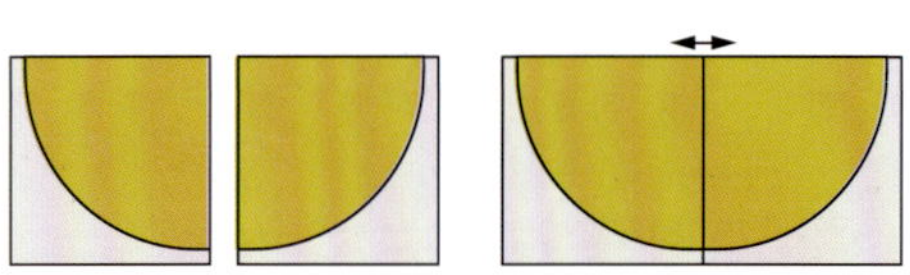

figure 3

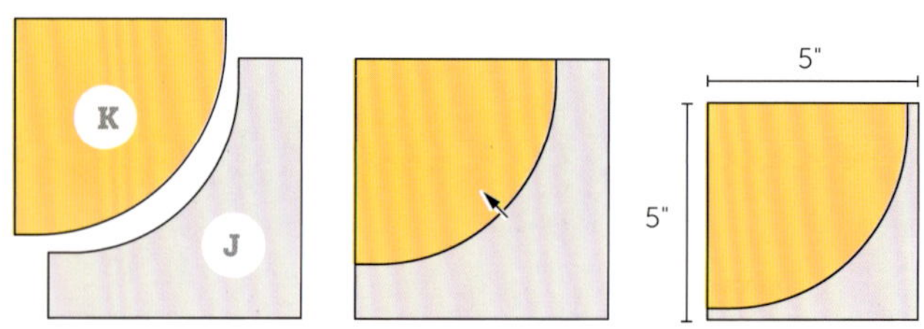

figure 4

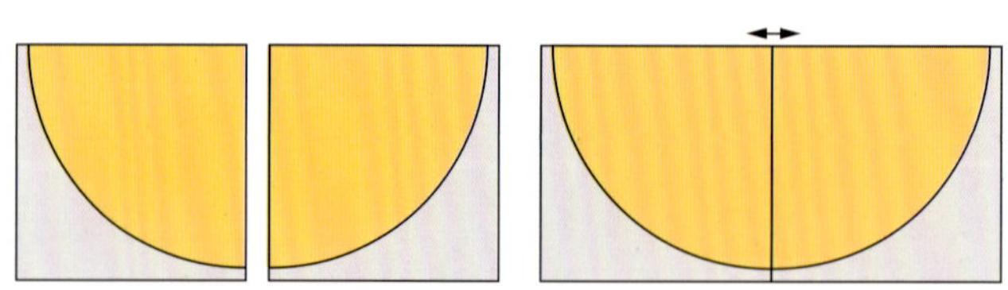

figure 5

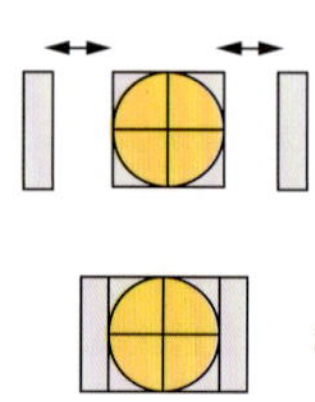

figure 6

MAKING THE COLUMNS

Assemble each of the 12 vertical columns of the quilt in order from left to right. Refer to the Paint Drip Construction Diagram for the correct orientation of the half-circle blocks.

1. To make Column 1, sew the lime green print strip 6.5" × 19" (16.5 × 48.5cm) to the top of the lime green/low volume print half-circle GH block.
   - Sew two lime green/low-volume print half-circle GH blocks together to make a circle. Sew this circle block to the top of the low-volume print strip 6½" × 41½" (16.5 × 105.4cm).
   - Sew together both pieces to complete Column 1.
2. To make Column 2, sew the yellow print strip 6½" × 35½" (16.5 × 90cm) to the top of a yellow/low-volume print half-circle GH block.
   - Sew the low-volume print strip 6½" × 53½" (16.5 × 136cm) to the top of a yellow/low-volume print half-circle GH block.
   - Sew together both pieces to complete Column 2.
3. To make Column 3, sew the yellow print strip 6½" × 15" (16.5 × 38cm) to the top of the low-volume print/yellow print half-circle GH block and the low-volume print strip 6½" × 77" (16.5 × 196cm) to the bottom.
4. To make Column 4, sew the yellow print strip 9½" × 38½" (24 × 96.5cm) to the top of the yellow print/low-volume print half-circle JK block. Sew the low-volume print strip 9½" × 3" (16.5 × 8cm) to the bottom.
   - Sew two yellow/low-volume print half-circle JK blocks together to make a circle. Sew this circle block to the top of the low-volume print strip 9½" × 13½" (24 × 34.5cm).
   - Sew two yellow/low-volume print half-circle GH blocks together to make a circle. On either side of the circle to the left and right, sew a low-volume print strip 2¼" × 6½" (6 × 16.5cm) **(fig. 6)**. Sew the low-volume strip 9½" × 21½" (24 × 55cm) to the bottom of the piece just made.
   - Sew together all three pieces to complete Column 4.

5. To make Column 5, sew the pink print strip 6½" × 60" (16.5 × 152.5cm) to the top of the pink print/low-volume print half-circle GH block.
   - Sew the low-volume print strip 6½" × 14" (16.5 × 36cm) to the top of the pink print/low-volume print half-circle GH block. Sew the low-volume print strip 6½" × 12½" (16.5 × 32cm) to the bottom.
   - Sew together both pieces to complete Column 5.

6. To make Column 6, sew the pink print strip 6½" × 26½" (16.5 × 67.5cm) to the top of the low-volume print/pink print half-circle GH block and the low-volume print strip 6½" × 65½" (16.5 × 166cm) to the bottom.

7. To make Column 7, refer to Figure 7.
   - Sew the low-volume print strip 6½" × 15" (16.5 × 38cm) to the low-volume print/pink print GH half-circle block. Then sew the pink print strip 3½" × 18" (9 × 45.5cm) to the right side.
   - Sew the pink print strip 9½" × 29½" (24 × 75cm) to the top of a large pink/low-volume half-circle JK block. Sew the low-volume print strip 9½" × 2" (24 × 5cm) to the bottom.
   - Sew two pink/low-volume print half-circle JK blocks together to make a circle. Sew this circle block to the top of the low-volume print strip 9½" × 28½" (24 × 72.5cm). Sew a large pink/low-volume half-circle JK block to the bottom. Sew together all three pieces to complete Column 7.

8. To make Column 8, sew the rust print strip 6½" × 73½" (16.5 × 186.7cm) to the top of the rust/low-volume print half-circle GH block and the low-volume print strip 6½" × 18½" (16.5 × 47cm) to the bottom.

9. To make Column 9, sew the light blue print strip 9½" × 40½" (24 × 103cm) to the top of the light blue/low-volume print half-circle JK block. Sew the low volume print strip 9½" × 3" (24 × 8cm) to the bottom.
   - Sew two light blue/low-volume print half-circle GH blocks together to make a circle. On either side of the circle to the left and right, sew a low-volume print strip 2¼" × 6½" (6 × 16.5cm) **(fig. 6)**. Sew the low-volume strip 9½" × 41½" (24 × 105.5cm) to the bottom of the piece just made.
   - Sew together both pieces to complete Column 9.

10. To make Column 10, sew the bright blue print strip 9½" × 26½" (24 × 67.5cm) to the top of the bright blue print/low-volume print half-circle JK block. Sew the low-volume print strip 9½" × 9½" (24 × 24.2cm) to the bottom.
   - Sew two bright blue/low-volume print half-circle JK blocks together to make a circle. Sew this circle block to the top of the low-volume print strip 9½" × 27" (24 × 69cm).
   - Sew two bright blue/low-volume print half-circle GH blocks together to make a circle. On either side of the circle to the left and right, sew a low-volume print strip 2¼" × 6½" (6 × 16.5cm) **(fig. 6)**. Sew the low-volume strip 9½" × 13½" (24 × 34.5cm) to the bottom of the piece just made.
   - Sew together all three pieces to complete Column 10.

11. To make Column 11, sew the bright blue print strip 6½" × 15" (16.5 × 38cm) to the top of the low-volume print/bright blue print half-circle GH block and the low-volume strip 6½" × 77" (16.5 × 196cm) to the bottom.

12. To make Column 12, sew the gray print strip 6½" ×50" (16.5 × 127cm) to the top of the bright blue print/low-volume print half-circle GH block.
   - Sew the low-volume print strip 6½" × 9½" (16.5 × 24.2cm) to the top of the bright blue print/low-volume print half-circle GH block. Sew the low-volume print strip 6½" × 27" (16.5 × 69cm) to the bottom.
   - Sew together both pieces to complete Column 12.

ASSEMBLING AND FINISHING

1. Sew together Columns 1–12 in order from left to right as shown in the Paint Drips Construction Diagram to complete your quilt top. Carefully match the top and bottom of each column to the next with pins first and then pin along the entire length of the rows. Press seams in one direction.

2. Refer to Finishing your Quilt (page 122) or use your favorite methods to layer and baste the quilt top, batting, and backing.

3. Quilt as desired. Longarm quilter Melissa Snyder quilted my quilt with a dripping popsicle pantograph I chose to mimic the bright colors and drips of the fabric design.

4. Bind your quilt using my French double-fold binding method as described in Binding (page 126) or your own method as preferred.

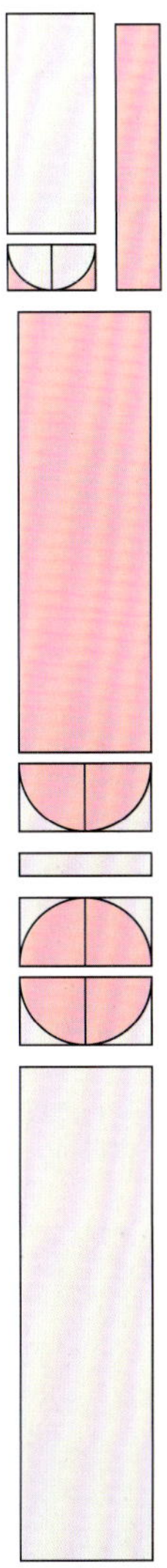

figure 7

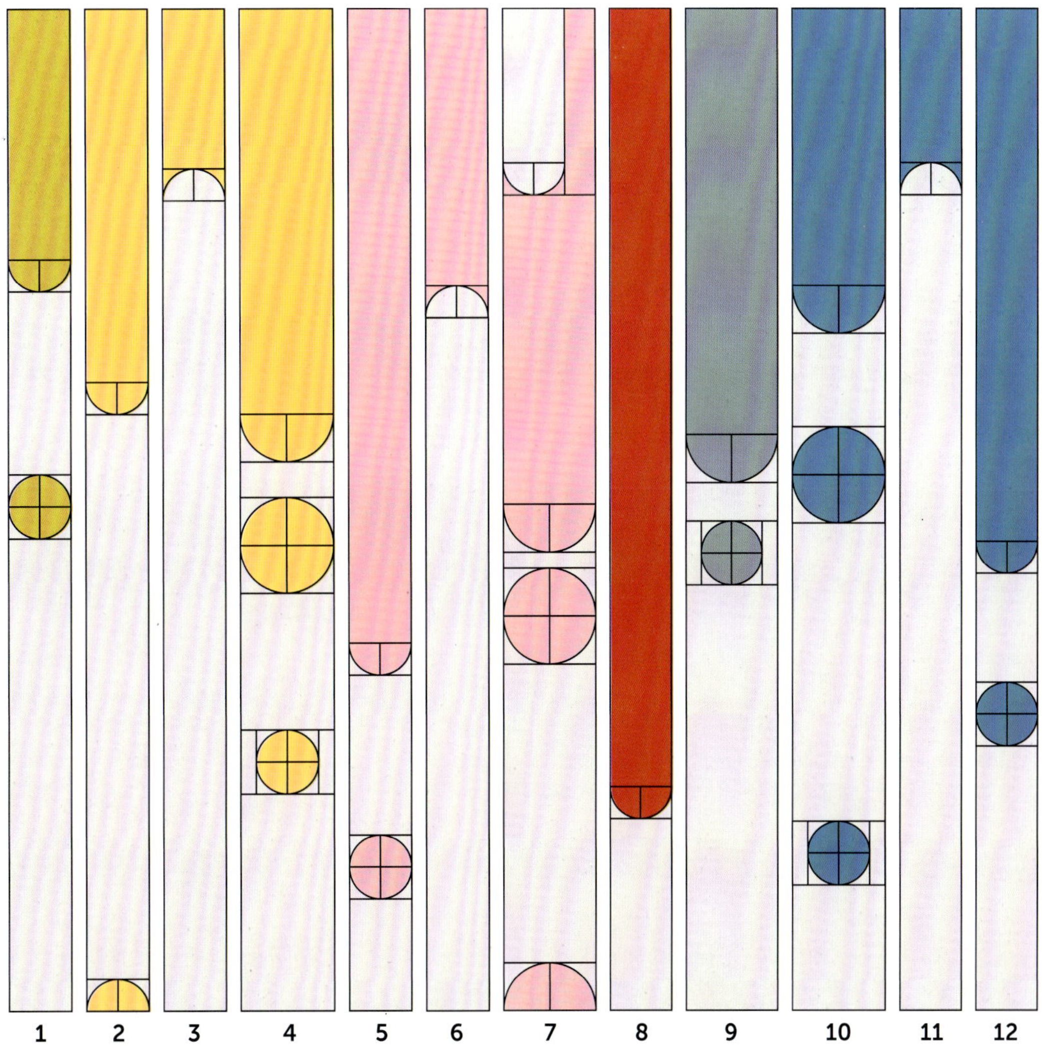

PAINT DRIPS CONSTRUCTION DIAGRAM

NINE PATCH CURVES QUILT

Finished size: 48" × 60" (122 × 152.5cm)
Designed, pieced, and quilted by Angela Pingel

Chances are, if you have made even one traditionally styled quilt, then you've used one of these two block designs. Here the Nine Patch and Drunkard's Path blocks are married together in a truly seamless design. In this beautifully scrappy quilt, the possibilities for color schemes are endless.

MATERIALS

Fabric amounts are based on yardage with a usable width of 42" (106.5cm). Fat quarters are 18" × 22" (45.5 × 56cm).

4 fat quarters assorted blue print fabrics

4 fat quarters assorted mint print fabrics

4 fat quarters assorted fuchsia print fabrics

4 fat quarters assorted gold print fabrics

3/8 yd (34.5cm) focal fabric for Nine Patch block centers*

8 assorted 1/4 yd (23cm) neutral print fabrics for template pieces

4 assorted 1/4 yd (23cm) neutral print fabrics for Nine Patch blocks

4 fat quarters assorted neutral print fabrics for Nine Patch blocks

3 1/3 yd (3m) backing fabric

1/2 yd (45.5cm) binding fabric

56" × 68" (142 × 173cm) batting

**I chose a print that combines the colors of the other fabrics in the quilt.*

TOOLS

Template patterns I and F

Template plastic or paper

CUTTING

WOF = width of fabric

FROM BLUE PRINT FABRICS:

- From 2 of the fabrics, cut 2 strips 4 1/2" × 18" (11.5 × 45.5cm) for a total of 4 strips. From the strips, cut 10 squares 4 1/2" × 4 1/2" (11.5 × 11.5cm). Cut 1 piece F from each square.
- From the remaining 2 fabrics, cut 2 strips 4 1/2" × 18" (11.5 × 45.5cm) for a total of 4 strips.

FROM MINT PRINT FABRICS:

- From 2 of the fabrics, cut 2 strips 4 1/2" × 18" (11.5 × 45.5cm) for a total of 4 strips. From the strips, cut 10 squares 4 1/2" × 4 1/2" (11.5 × 11.5cm). Cut 1 piece F from each square.
- From the remaining 2 fabrics, cut 2 strips 4 1/2 × 18" (11.5 × 45.5cm) for a total of 4 strips.

continued on next page

FROM FUCHSIA PRINT FABRICS:

- From 2 of the fabrics, cut 2 strips 4½" × 18" (11.5 × 45.5cm) for a total of 4 strips. From the strips, cut 10 squares 4½" × 4½" (11.5 × 11.5cm). Cut 1 piece F from each square.
- From the remaining 2 fabrics, cut 2 strips 4½" × 18" (11.5 × 45.5cm) for a total of 4 strips.

FROM GOLD PRINT FABRICS:

- From 2 of the fabrics, cut 2 strips 4½" × 18" (11.5 × 45.5cm) for a total of 4 strips. From the strips, cut 10 squares 4½" × 4½" (11.5 × 11.5cm). Cut 1 piece F from each square.
- From the remaining 2 fabrics, cut 2 strips 4½" × 18" (11.5 × 45.5cm) for a total of 4 strips.

FROM FOCAL FABRIC FOR NINE PATCH BLOCK CENTERS:

- Cut 2 strips 4½" (11.5cm) × WOF.

FROM TEMPLATE NEUTRAL PRINT FABRICS:

- From 8 pieces ¼ yd (23cm), cut 1 strip 6½" (16.5cm) × WOF for a total of 8 strips. Cut 5 squares 6½" × 6½" (16.5 × 16.5cm) from each strip. Cut 1 piece I from each square.

FROM NINE-PATCH NEUTRAL FABRICS:

- From 4 fat quarter pieces, cut 2 strips 4½" × 18" (11.5 × 45.5cm) for a total of 8 strips.
- From 4 pieces ¼ yd (23cm), cut 1 strip 4½" (11.5cm) × WOF for a total of 4 strips.

FROM BACKING FABRIC:

- Cut 2 pieces 1⅔ yd (1.5m) × WOF.

FROM BINDING FABRIC:

- Cut 6 strips 2½" (6.5cm) × WOF.

TIP

Make this quilt more scrappy or less scrappy in a snap. All assorted neutral fabrics can be one fabric, or they can all be different scraps. The choice is yours!

MAKING THE BLOCKS

Unfinished block size: 12½" × 12½" (31.5 × 31.5cm)
This quilt has 10 Nine Patch blocks and 10 Drunkard's Path curved blocks.

DRUNKARD'S PATH CURVED BLOCKS

1. Sew together the curved pieces K and H **(fig. 1)** as follows:

- Sew 10 blue print pieces F to 10 neutral print pieces I.
- Sew 10 fuchsia print pieces F to 10 neutral print pieces I.
- Sew 10 mint print pieces F to 10 neutral print pieces I.
- Sew 10 gold print pieces F to 10 neutral print pieces I.

Press the seams toward the H pieces. Trim the blocks to 6½" × 6½" (16.5 × 16.5cm). You will have a total of 40 quarter-circle units.

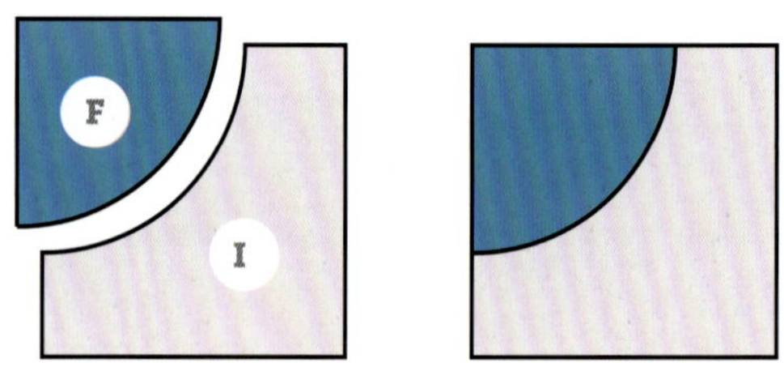

figure 1

2. Sew each gold/neutral unit to the left of a mint/neutral unit, matching neutral sides. Press the seams open. Sew a blue/neutral unit to the left of a fuchsia/neutral unit, matching the neutral sides **(fig. 2)**. Press the seams open.

figure 2

figure 3

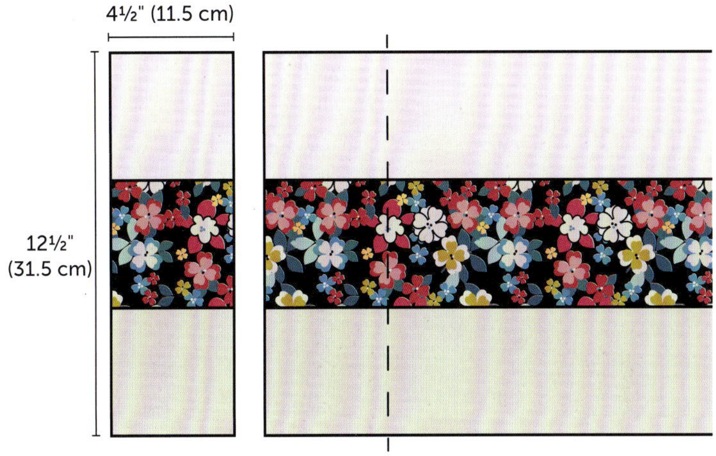

figure 4

3. Sew the gold/mint unit to the blue/fuchsia unit, matching the neutral fabrics and the center seams. Repeat 3 more times to create 4 blocks total.

4. Sew a gold/neutral unit to the right of a mint/neutral unit, matching neutral sides. Press the seams open. Sew a blue/neutral unit to the right of a fuchsia/neutral unit, matching the neutral sides. Press the seams open.

5. Sew the mint/gold unit to the fuchsia/blue unit, matching the neutral fabrics and the center seam. Repeat 5 more times to create 6 blocks total.

NINE PATCH BLOCKS

1. Sew a neutral fabric strip 4½" (11.5cm) × WOF to either side of a focal strip 4½" × WOF **(fig. 3)**. Press the seams toward the focal strip. Repeat to create a second strip set.

2. Cross-cut each pieced strip set into 5 strips 4½" × 12½" (11.5 × 31.5cm) for a total of 10 pieces **(fig. 4)**.

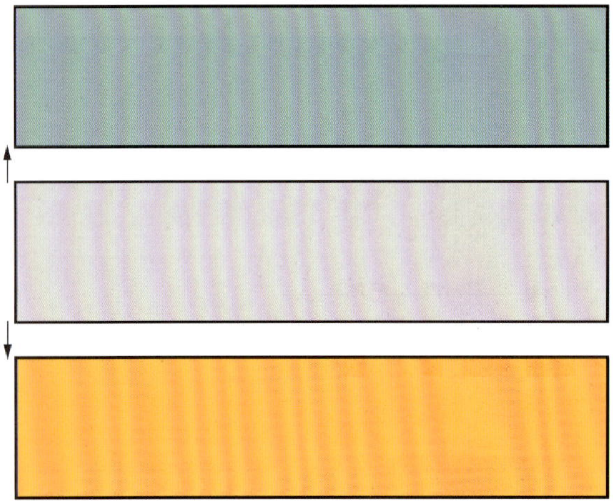

figure 5

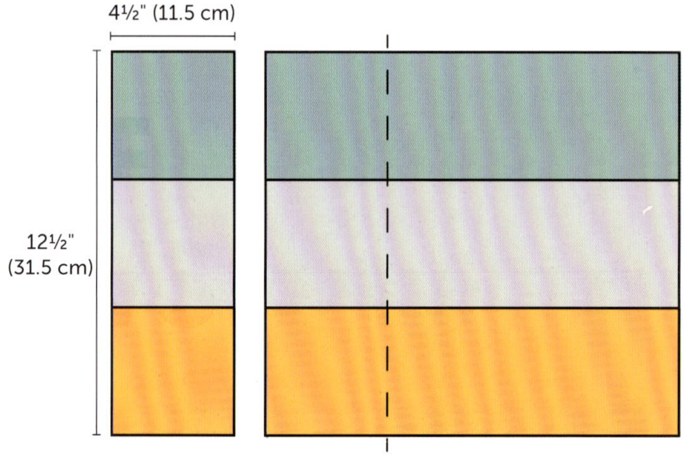

figure 6

figure 7

3. Sew a colored strip 4½" × 18" (11.5 × 45.5cm) to each side of a neutral print strip 4½" × 18" (11.5 × 45.5cm) **(fig. 5)** as follows:

- Sew 2 strips with mint and gold.
- Sew 2 strips with blue and gold.
- Sew 2 strips with blue and fuchsia.
- Sew 2 strips with mint and fuchsia.

Press the seams toward the colored strips.

4. Cross-cut the pieced strip set from Step 3 into strips 4½" × 12½" (11.5 × 31.5cm) **(fig. 6)** as follows:

- Cut 6 strips with mint and gold.
- Cut 4 strips with blue and gold.
- Cut 6 strips with blue and fuchsia.
- Cut 4 strips with mint and fuchsia.

5. Assemble the Nine Patch block in three rows of strips 4½" × 12½" (11.5 × 31.5cm). The middle row is always a neutral/focal/neutral strip. The top and bottom rows always match in groups of two colors, but the colors alternate left to right **(fig. 7)**. Assemble as follows:

- Sew 3 blocks with mint and gold.
- Sew 2 blocks with blue and gold.
- Sew 3 blocks with blue and fuchsia.
- Sew 2 blocks with mint and fuchsia.

Press the seams in one direction. You will have a total of 10 Nine Patch blocks.

MAKING THE QUILT TOP

1. Arrange the blocks into five rows of four alternating blocks each, as shown in the Nine Patch Curves Construction Diagram. Rotate the blocks as necessary for color placement. Sew together the two Nine Patch blocks and two Drunkard's Path blocks in each row. Press the seams toward the Nine Patch blocks. Construct rows 1 through 5.

2. Sew the rows together to make the quilt top. Press the seams in one direction.

FINISHING

1. Refer to Finishing Your Quilt (page 122) or use your favorite methods to layer and baste the quilt top, batting, and backing.

2. Quilt as desired. I quilted an allover swirling pattern that adds movement to the quilt top.

3. Bind your quilt using my French double-fold binding method as described in Binding (page 126) or your own preferred method.

TIP

Because this quilt is based on two blocks, the size is limited only by the number of blocks you want to make. You can easily make this quilt larger by adding extra rows and columns. It's the perfect way to use your scraps!

NINE PATCH CURVES CONSTRUCTION DIAGRAM

CAT EYE QUILT

Finished size: 47" × 62" (119.4 × 157.5cm)
Designed and pieced by Angela Pingel
Quilted By Marion McClellan

Can you see the cats' eyes? You may need to squint and turn the page sideways, but that is all I can see with this particular layout. The hallmark of the curved pieces in this design is using them sparingly and as negative space. What would otherwise be a simple but fabulous scrappy patchwork quilt on point, takes on more interest with sections of the design "cut out" with curves. This is the perfect quilt for using stash and scrap fabrics. Each print fabric can be made from a unique piece of fabric if you choose. Or you can tighten the palette and stick with a fat quarter bundle of a single collection.

MATERIALS

21 fat quarters (46 × 56cm) print fabric
1½ yds (137cm) white fabric
4 yd (366cm) backing fabric
½ yd (68.5cm) binding fabric
50" × 68" (127 × 173cm) batting

TOOLS

Template patterns N and O
Template plastic or paper

CUTTING:

WOF = width of fabric

FROM FAT QUARTER PRINT FABRIC:

- Cut 34 squares 6" × 6" (15.5 × 15.5cm).
- Cut 62 squares 7" × 7" (18 × 18cm).
  - Subcut 14 squares 7" × 7" (18 × 18cm) along the diagonal into 28 Half Square Triangles.
  - Subcut 48 squares 7" × 7" (18 × 18cm) into 48 pieces N.

FROM WHITE FABRIC:

- Cut 8 strips 6" (15.5cm) × WOF.
  - Subcut each strip into six 6" × 6" (15.5 × 15.5cm) squares for a total of 48 squares.
  - Cut 48 pieces O from these squares.

FROM BINDING FABRIC:

- Cut 6 strips 2¼" (5.7cm) × WOF.

FROM BACKING FABRIC:

- Cut 2 rectangles 72" (183cm) × WOF.

NOTE

These squares can all comfortably be cut from 21 fat quarters, but to ensure this, cut the 7" × 7" (18 × 18cm) squares first from the fat quarters and then the 6" × 6" (15.5 × 15.5cm) squares. You will need to cut up to three 7" × 7" (18 × 18cm) squares and up to two 6" × 6" (15.5 × 15.5cm) from most fat quarters.

MAKING THE QUILT BLOCK UNITS

1. Begin by making the quarter-circle units. Sew together the small curved pieces N and O as follows.
   - Sew 48 white pieces O to 48 color print pieces N. Press the seams toward piece O. Trim each unit to 6" x 6" (15.5 x 15.5cm) leaving a ¼" (6mm) seam allowance on the N piece **(fig. 1)**. You will have a total of 48 quarter-circle NO units.

2. Sew the units from Step 1 into pairs in the orientation shown to make 24 pieces **(fig. 2)**. Press towards the white fabric.

3. Sew the units from Step 2 in pairs in the orientation shown to make twelve curved four-patch blocks **(fig. 2)**. Press all seams open. These pieces will now be called curved four-patch blocks.

4. Sew 24 print squares 6" x 6" (15.5 x 15.5cm) into 12 pairs. Press seams in one direction. Sew each pair to another pair to create six four-patch blocks **(fig. 3)**. Press seams open. These pieces will now be called four-patch blocks.

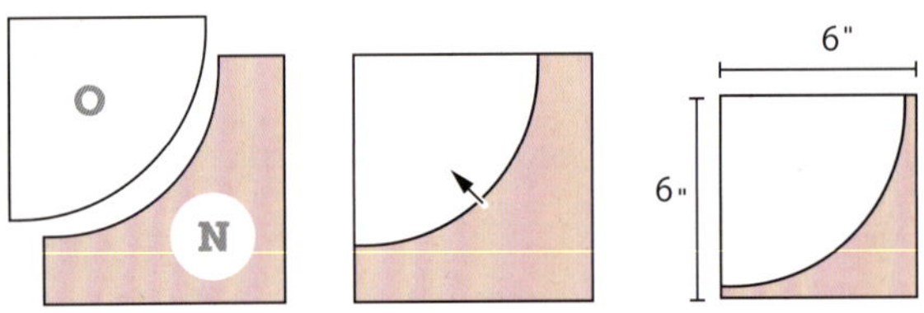

figure 1

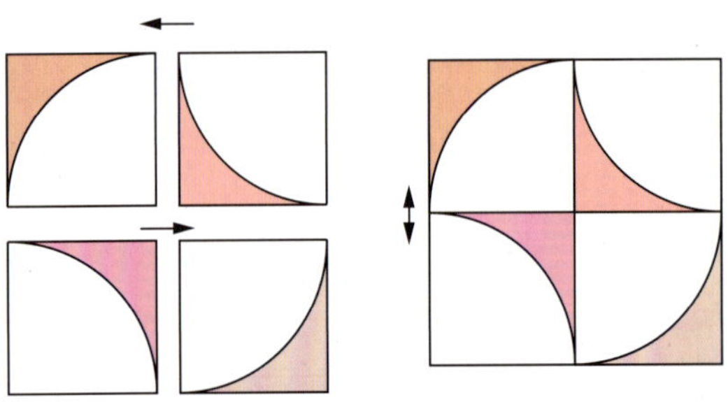

figure 2

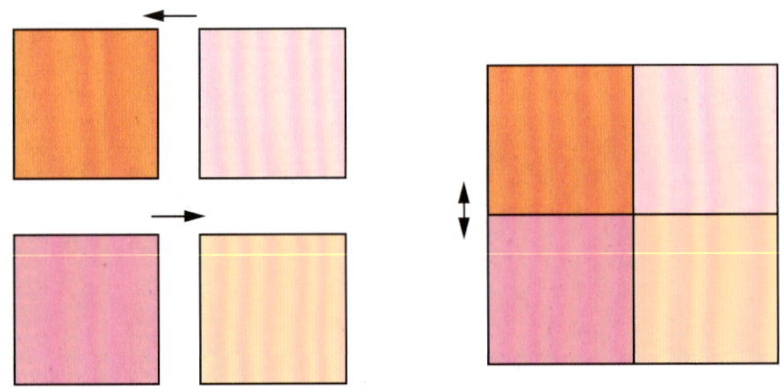

figure 3

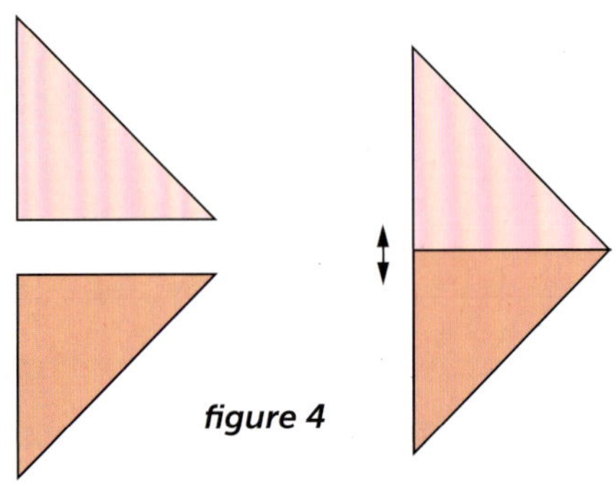

figure 4

TIP

Keep the quilt visually simple by sticking to fabrics in a grouping of analogous colors. This provides some interest while preventing the eye from bouncing everywhere at once.

5. Sew eight HST print pieces into four pairs along their shorter straight edges as shown **(fig. 4)**. Press seams open. These pieces will now be called triangle units.

6. Sew 10 print squares 6" × 6" (15.5 × 15.5cm) to 10 HST print pieces aligning top edges as shown **(fig. 5)**. Press seams toward squares and trim excess points along the bottom of the squares.

7. Sew the units from Step 6 to the remaining 10 HST print prices aligning left edges as shown **(fig. 6)**. Press seams toward the triangles. These pieces will now be called triangle square units.

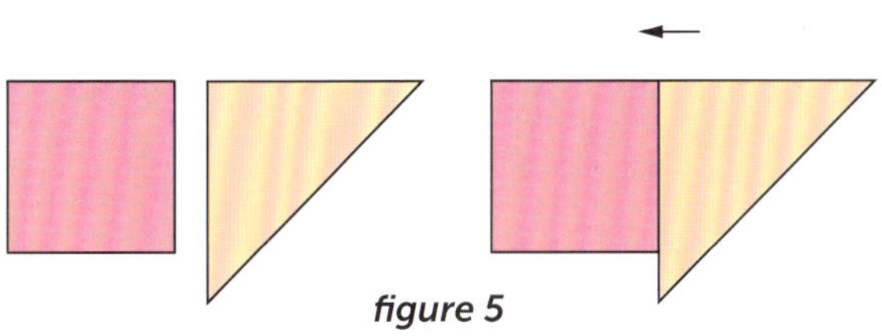

figure 5

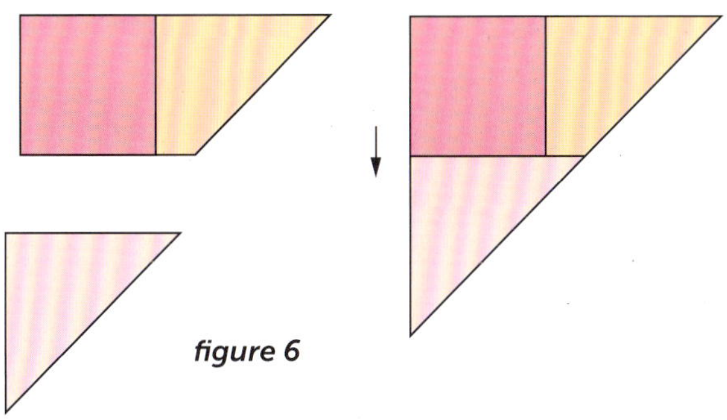

figure 6

ASSEMBLE THE QUILT TOP

Refer to the Cat Eye Construction Diagram for assembly of the quilt block units created in the previous section.

1. Create two short diagonal rows with one curved four-patch block and two triangle square units together as shown along the 11½" (29cm) edges, aligning center points, and alternating blocks. This creates rows 2 and 7.
2. Create two medium diagonal rows with two curved four-patch blocks, one four patch block, and two triangle square units together as shown along the 11½" (29cm) edges, aligning center points, and alternating blocks. This creates rows 3 and 6.

CAT EYE CONSTRUCTION DIAGRAM

3. Create two long diagonal rows with 3 curved four patch blocks, 2 four patch blocks, 1 triangle square unit and 1 triangle unit together as shown along the 11½" (29cm) edges aligning center points, alternating blocks. This creates rows 4 and 5.

4. Sew the six diagonal pieced rows created in Steps 1–3 along with the two remaining triangle units to one another in order as guided by the Construction Diagram. Be sure to align and match center points of each block in each row and pin in place before sewing each row.

FINISHING

1. Refer to Finishing your Quilt (page 122) or use your favorite methods to layer and baste the quilt top, batting, and backing.

2. Quilt as desired. Longarm quilter Marion McClellan quilted my quilt with an all-over free motion loop design.

3. Bind your quilt using my French double-fold binding method as described in Binding (page 126) or your own method as preferred.

CAT EYE QUILT DIAGRAM

FLOWER POWER QUILT

Finished size: 70" × 84" (178 × 213cm)
Designed, pieced, and quilted by Angela Pingel

Come join the movement with this Flower Power quilt. A fresh, updated version of times long gone by, this modular pattern plays on two sizes of flowers. The two combine in an offset pattern that keeps your eye moving. Pull out your AccuQuilt cutter and both die sizes for this one, and you will have your fabric cut in no time!

MATERIALS

Fabric amounts are based on yardage with a usable width of 42" (106.5cm). Fat quarters are 18" × 22" (45.5 × 56cm).

1 yd (91.5cm) dark gray print fabric

1 yd (91.5cm) aqua print fabric

1 yd (91.5cm) green print fabric

1 yd (91.5cm) pink print fabric

1 fat quarter light gray solid fabric

1 fat quarter aqua solid fabric

1 fat quarter green solid fabric

1 fat quarter orange solid fabric

4. yd (4m) white solid fabric

5⅛ yd (4.7m) backing fabric

⅔ yd (61cm) binding fabric

78" × 92" (198 × 234cm) batting

TOOLS

Template patterns A, B, C, and D or 3½" (9cm) and 7" (18cm) AccuQuilt dies and cutter (page 14)

Template plastic or paper (if using patterns)

CUTTING

WOF = width of fabric

FROM DARK GRAY PRINT FABRIC:

- Cut 3 strips 6½" (16.5cm) × WOF.
  Cut 18 pieces D from the strips.
- Cut 1 strip 6" (15cm) × WOF.
  Cut 6 squares 6" × 6" (15 × 15cm).

FROM AQUA PRINT FABRIC:

- Cut 3 strips 6½" (16.5cm) × WOF.
  Cut 18 pieces F from the strips.
- Cut 1 strip 6" (15cm) × WOF.
  Cut 6 squares 6" × 6" (15 × 15cm).

FROM GREEN PRINT FABRIC:

- Cut 3 strips 6½" (16.5cm) × WOF.
  Cut 18 pieces D from the strips.
- Cut 1 strip 6" (15cm) × WOF.
  Cut 6 squares 6" × 6" (15 × 15cm).

continued on next page

FROM PINK PRINT FABRIC:

- Cut 3 strips 6½" (16.5cm) × WOF. Cut 18 pieces D from the strips.
- Cut 1 strip 6" (15cm) × WOF. Cut 6 squares 6" × 6" (15 × 15cm).

FROM LIGHT GRAY SOLID FABRIC:

- Cut 5 strips 3½" × 18" (9 × 45.5cm). Cut 18 pieces B from the strips.
- Cut 1 strip 3" × 18" (7.5 × 45.5cm). Cut 6 squares 3" × 3" (7.5 × 7.5cm).

FROM AQUA SOLID FABRIC:

- Cut 5 strips 3½" × 18" (9 × 45.5cm). Cut 18 pieces B from the strips.
- Cut 1 strip 3" × 18" (7.5 × 45.5cm). Cut 6 squares 3" × 3" (7.5 × 7.5cm).

FROM GREEN SOLID FABRIC:

- Cut 5 strips 3½" × 18" (9 × 45.5cm). Cut 18 pieces B from the strips.
- Cut 1 strip 3" × 18" (7.5 × 45.5cm). Cut 6 squares 3" × 3" (7.5 × 7.5cm).

FROM ORANGE SOLID FABRIC:

- Cut 5 strips 3½" × 18" (9 × 45.5cm). Cut 18 pieces B from the strips.
- Cut 1 strip 3" × 18" (7.5 × 45.5cm). Cut 6 squares 3" × 3" (7.5 × 7.5cm).

FROM WHITE SOLID FABRIC:

- Cut 1 strip 6" (15cm) × WOF. Cut the strip into 18 strips 2" × 6" (5 × 15cm).
- Cut 1 strip 7½" (19cm) × WOF. Cut the strip into 18 strips 2" × 7½" (5 × 19cm).
- Cut 1 strip 4" (10cm) × WOF. Cut the strip into 18 strips 1½" × 4" (3.8 × 10cm).
- Cut 1 strip 3" (7.5cm) × WOF. Cut the strip into 18 strips 1½" × 3" (3.8 × 7.5cm).
- Cut 15 strips 8½" (21.5cm) × WOF. Cut the strips into 72 squares 8½" × 8½" (21.5 × 21.5cm). Cut 1 piece C from each square. Use the large scrap pieces left from cutting pieces C to cut 72 pieces A.

FROM BACKING FABRIC:

- Cut 2 rectangles 92" (234cm) × WOF.

FROM BINDING FABRIC:

- Cut 8 strips 2½" (6.5cm) × WOF.

MAKING THE BLOCKS

This quilt has 24 small petal blocks and 24 large petal blocks, each of which is a quarter of the flower patterning. All the blocks are constructed in the same manner.

SMALL PETAL BLOCKS (FOUR PETALS TOGETHER)

Unfinished block size: 14½" × 14½" (37 × 37cm)
Make six.

1. Sew together curved pieces A and B **(fig. 1)** as follows:
   - Sew 18 white solid pieces A to 18 light gray solid pieces B.
   - Sew 18 white solid pieces A to 18 aqua solid pieces B.
   - Sew 18 white solid pieces A to 18 green solid pieces B.
   - Sew 18 white solid pieces A to 18 orange print pieces B.

   Press the seams toward piece B. You will have a total of 72 quarter-circle units.

2. Sew a white solid strip 1½" × 3" (3.8 x7.5cm) to the bottom of a solid color square 3" × 3" (7.5 × 7.5cm). Press the seam toward the square. Sew a white solid strip 1½" × 4" (3.8 × 10cm) to the left side. Press the seam toward the white solid strip **(fig. 2)**. Make six units with a light gray solid square, six with an aqua solid square, six with a green solid square, and six with an orange solid square.

3. Sew together the quarter-circle units from Step 1 to make six matching pairs in each color **(fig. 3)**. Press all seams open. You have six quarter-circle units unused.

4. Sew the remaining six quarter-circle units from Step 1 to the matching units from Step 2 **(fig. 4)**. Press all seams open.

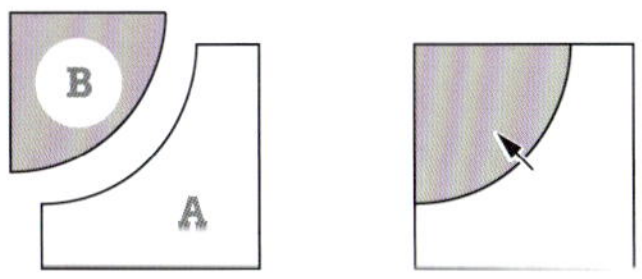

figure 1

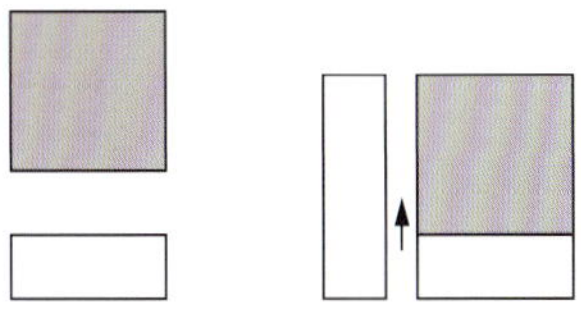

figure 2

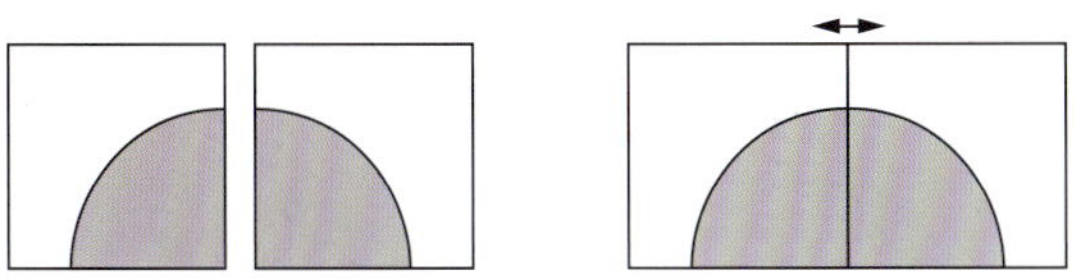

figure 3

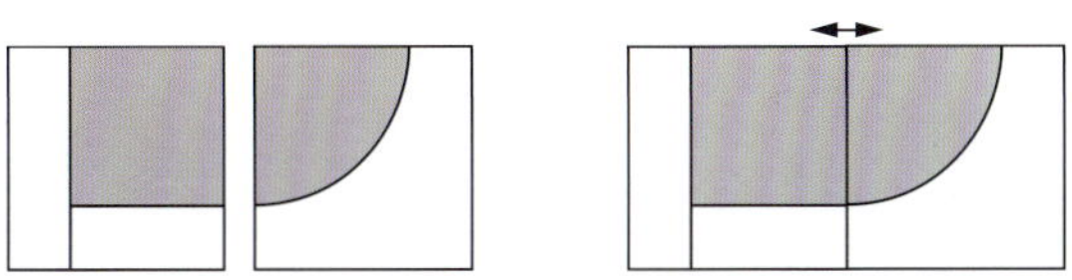

figure 4

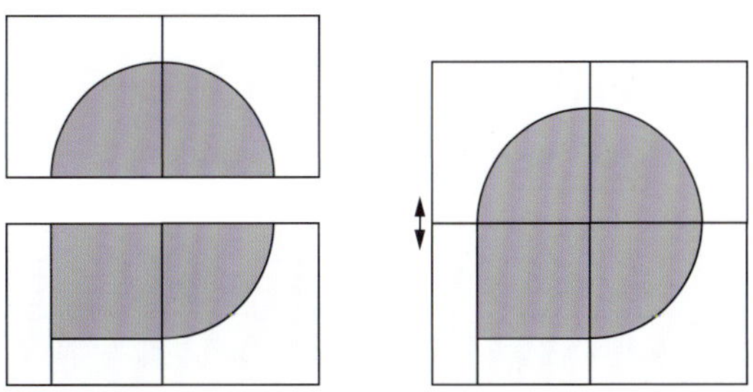

figure 5

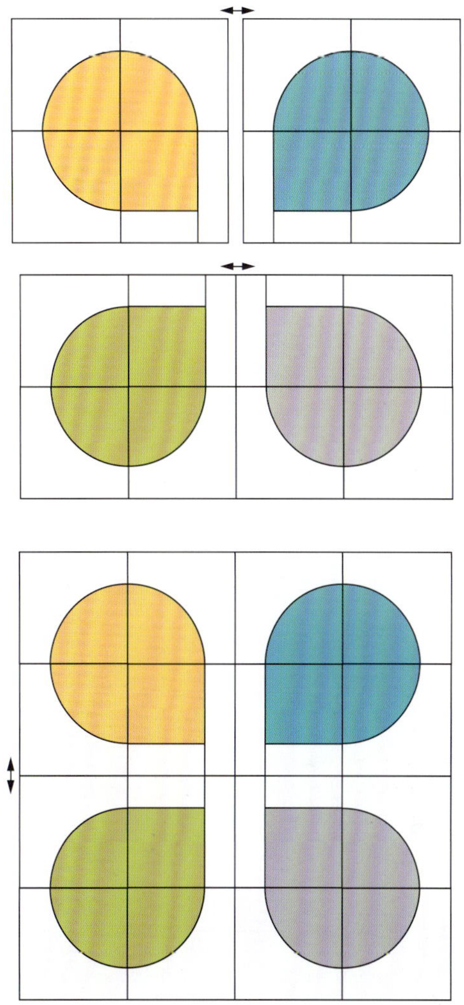

figure 6

5. Assemble the units of matching colors from Steps 3 and 4, aligning center points **(fig. 5)**. You will have six white/light gray units, six white/aqua units, six white/green units, and six white/orange units. Press all seams open.

6. To complete the small petal blocks, assemble the units from Step 5, matching seams in the center **(fig. 6)**. Sew each orange unit to an aqua unit, and each green unit to a light gray unit. Press the seams open. Then sew each orange/aqua unit to a green/light gray unit to form the small petal block. Press the seams open. Square up the blocks to 14½" × 14½" (37 × 37cm).

LARGE PETAL BLOCKS (SINGLE PETAL)

Unfinished block size: 14½" × 14½" (37 × 37cm)
Make 24.
Follow the same basic directions as in Steps 1–5 for the small petal blocks.

1. Sew together curved pieces C and D as follows:
   - Sew 18 white solid pieces C to 18 dark gray print pieces D.
   - Sew 18 white solid pieces C to 18 aqua print pieces D.
   - Sew 18 white solid pieces C to 18 green print pieces D.
   - Sew 18 white solid pieces C to 18 pink print pieces D.

   Press the seams toward piece D. You will have a total of 72 quarter-circle units.

2. Sew a white solid strip 2" × 6" (5 × 15cm) to the bottom of a color print square 6" × 6" (15 × 15cm). Press the seam toward the square. Sew a white solid strip 2" × 7½" (5 × 19cm) to the left side. Press the seam toward the white solid strip. Make six units with a dark gray print square, six units with an aqua print square, six units with a green print square, and six units with a pink print square.

3. Sew together the quarter-circle units from Step 1 to make 24 matching pairs. Press all seams open. You will have 24 quarter-circle units unused.

4. Sew the remaining quarter-circle units from Step 1 to the matching units from Step 2. Press all seams open.

5. To complete the large petal blocks, assemble the units of matching colors from Steps 3 and 4, matching seams in the center. Press all seams open. You will have six dark gray print/white solid blocks, six aqua print/white solid blocks, six green print/white solid blocks, and six pink print/white solid blocks. Trim the blocks to 14½" × 14½" (37 × 37cm).

MAKING THE QUILT TOP

1. Refer to the Flower Power Construction Diagram to sew together the quilt top in six rows of five blocks each, aligning adjacent seams. Press all seams open.

2. Sew the rows together aligning adjacent seams to complete the quilt top. Press all seams in one direction.

FINISHING

1. Refer to Finishing Your Quilt (page 122) or use your favorite methods to layer and baste the quilt top, batting, and backing.

2. Quilt as desired. I quilted an allover meandering pattern that adds texture to the quilt top.

3. Bind your quilt using my French double-fold binding method as described in Binding (page 126) or your own preferred method.

FLOWER POWER CONSTRUCTION DIAGRAM

FULL BLOOM QUILT

Finished size: 74½" × 74½" (189 × 189cm)
Designed and pieced by Angela Pingel
Quilted by Melissa Snyder of Longarm Louise

As soon as you start playing with curves and squares, a leaf or flower pattern emerges. Highly stylized, this quilt is perfect for those who don't want anything too flowery. Experiment with colors and arrangement to create your perfect garden. Use only one of the two blocks and make a completely new design, or drop the sashing for an even more modern look. Simple changes have a big impact on this design. Interestingly, this quilt pattern is the first time I have ever altered the curved piece after it is sewn. That little square sewn to the corner of the quarter circle block creates a whole new world of design options.

MATERIALS

Fabric amounts are based on yardage with a usable width of 42" (106.5cm).

4½ yds (412cm) background fabric

1½ yds (137cm) pink print fabric

2¼ yds (20cm) green print fabric

⅜ yd (34.3cm) yellow print fabric

⅛ yd (11.5cm) black fabric

4½ yds (411.5cm) backing fabric

⅝ yd (57cm) binding fabric

78" × 78" (198 × 198cm) batting

TOOLS

Template patterns C and D

Template plastic or paper

CUTTING

WOF = width of fabric

FROM BACKGROUND FABRIC:

- For blocks
  - Cut 18 strips 6" (15.5cm) × WOF.
  - Subcut each strip into 5 squares 6" × 6" (15.5 × 15.5cm) for a total of 126 squares.
  - Cut 108 pieces C from the squares and discard two squares, keeping 16 squares 6" × 6" (15.5 × 15.5cm).
- For sashing
  - Cut 2 strips 22½" (56cm) × WOF.
  - Subcut one strip into 16 strips 22½" × 2½" (56 × 6.5cm) and the second strip into 8 strips 22½" × 2½" (56 × 6.5cm) for a total of 24 strips 22½" × 2½" (56 × 6.5cm). Discard extra fabric from the second strip.

TIP

Cutting piece C results in a large amount of discarded fabric. Try trimming this inner curve down to a usable 4" × 4" (10 × 10cm) square for use in another project.

continued on next page

FROM PINK PRINT FABRIC:

- Cut 7 strips 6" (15.5cm) × WOF.
  - Subcut each strip into 7 squares 6" × 6" (15.5 × 15.5cm) for a total of 49 squares. Cut 48 pieces D from the squares and discard 1 square.

FROM GREEN PRINT FABRIC:

- Cut 12 strips 6" (15.5cm) × WOF.
  - Subcut each strip into 7 squares 6" × 6" (15.5 × 15.5cm) for a total of 84 squares. Cut 60 pieces D from the squares and discard 4 squares keeping 20 squares 6" × 6" (15.5 × 15.5cm).

FROM YELLOW PRINT FABRIC:

- Cut 1 strip 2½" (6.5cm) × WOF.
  - Subcut 16 squares 2½" × 2½" (6.5 × 6.5cm) from the strip.
- Cut 2 strips 4" (10cm) × WOF.
  - Subcut each strip into 8 squares 4" × 4" (10 × 10cm) for a total of 16 squares.

FROM BLACK FABRIC:

- Cut 2 strips 1¾" (4.5cm) × WOF.
  - Subcut one strip into 24 squares 1¾" × 1¾" (4.5 × 4.5cm) and the second strip into 12 squares 1¾" × 1¾" (4.5 × 4.5cm) for a total of 36 squares 1¾" × 1¾" (4.5 × 4.5cm). Discard extra fabric from the second strip.

FROM BACKING FABRIC:

- Cut 2 pieces 2¼ yd (206cm) × WOF.

FROM BINDING FABRIC:

- Cut 8 strips 2¼" (6cm) × WOF.

MAKING THE BLOCKS

LEAF BLOCKS

Unfinished block size: 22½" × 22½" (56 × 56cm)

The quilt top has five leaf blocks each made with four leaflet blocks.

1. Sew each green print piece D to background piece C. Press the seams toward piece D. Trim each unit to 6" × 6" (15.5 × 15.5cm) leaving a ¼" (6mm) seam allowance on the C piece **(fig. 1)**. You will have a total of 60 quarter-circle CD units with green D.

2. Sew each green print 6" × 6" (15.5 × 15.5cm) square to an CD unit made in Step 1 in the orientation shown **(fig. 2)** for a total of 20 square/circle strips. Press seams toward the squares.

3. Sew the remaining 40 units from Step 1 into pairs to make 20 half-circle units **(fig. 2)**. Press all seams open or to the right piece.

4. Sew the units made in Step 2 and Step 3 together in the orientation shown **(fig. 2)** for a total of 20 leaflet blocks.

5. Sew a black 1¾" × 1¾" (4.5 × 4.5cm) square along the diagonal to each leaflet block in the bottom right-hand corner curve in the orientation shown **(fig. 3)**. Flip and fold half of the square to align with the edges of the block. Trim away the excess black and background fabric from the back of the quilt leaving a ¼" (6mm) seam allowance. Press the seam toward the background fabric. You will have a total of 20 leaflet blocks with a small black flip and fold corner.

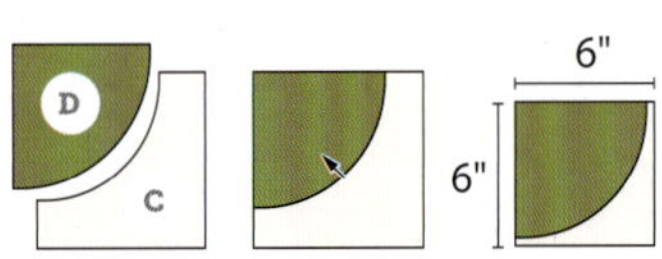

figure 1

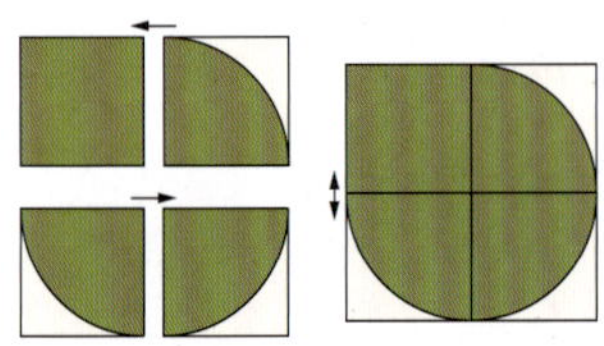

figure 2

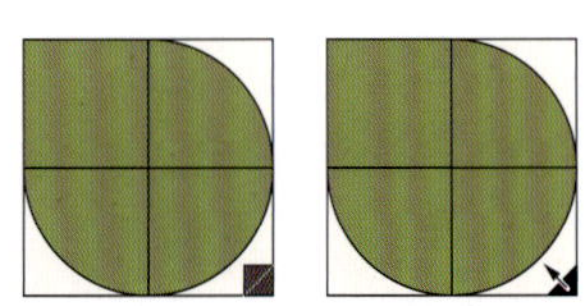

figure 3

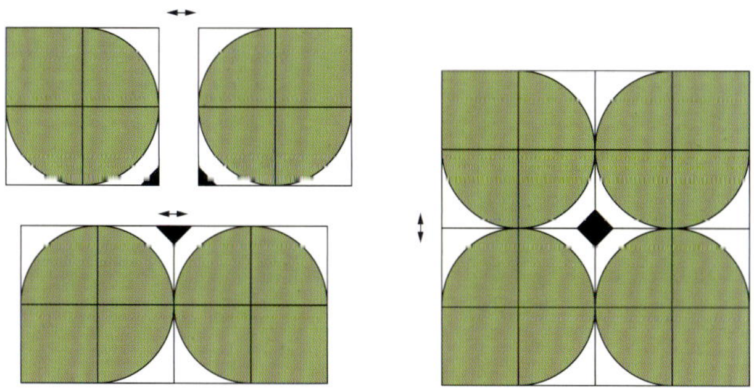

figure 4

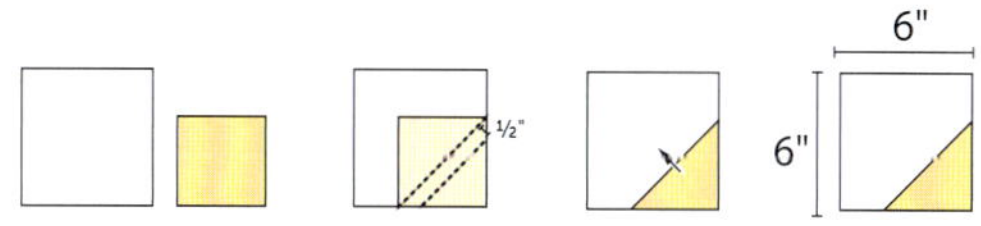

figure 5

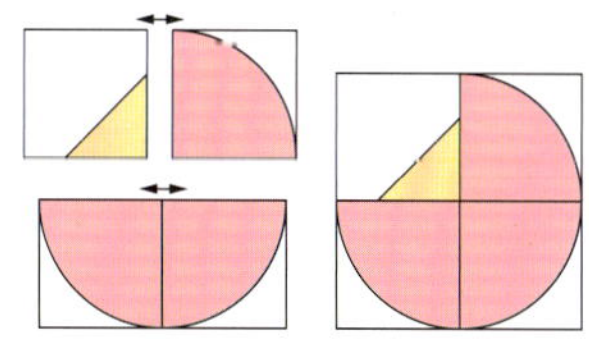

figure 6

6. Sew the leaflet blocks created in Step 5 together into pairs in the orientation shown, matching center and corner seams. Press the seams open. You will have a total of 10 pairs of leaflet blocks **(fig. 4)**.

7. Sew each leaflet pair created in Step 6 to another in the orientation shown to create the leaf blocks. Again, match center and corner seams and press the seams open. You will have a total of five leaf blocks **(fig. 4)**.

PETAL BLOCKS

Unfinished block size: 22½" × 22½" (56 × 56cm)
The quilt top has four flower blocks each made with four petal blocks.

1. Sew each pink print piece D to background piece C. Press the seams toward piece D. Trim each unit to 6" × 6" (15.5 × 15.5cm) leaving a ¼" (6mm) seam allowance on the C piece **(fig. 1)**. You will have a total of 48 quarter-circle CD units with pink D.

> **TIP**
>
> Before trimming the excess corner triangle fabric away from the block, sew a line parallel to the diagonal seam ½" (12.7mm) away toward the corner. If you trim with the ¼" (6mm) seam allowance, you will be left with a small square of two triangles in yellow print and background fabric for another project **(fig. 5)**.

2. Place the yellow print fabric 4" × 4" (10 × 10cm) square right sides together with the background 6" × 6" (15.5 × 15.5cm) square aligning two edges together. Sew along the diagonal from corner to corner of the yellow square. Flip and fold half of the yellow square to align with the edges of the background block. Trim away the excess yellow and background fabric from the back of the quilt leaving a ¼" (6mm) seam allowance. Press the seam toward the background fabric **(fig. 5)**. You will have a total of 16 yellow print/ background fabric squares now known as yellow triangle squares.

3. Sew each yellow triangle 6" × 6" (15.5 × 15.5cm) square created in Step 2 to a cd unit made in Step 1 in the orientation shown **(fig. 6)** for a total of 16 triangle square/circle strips. Press seams toward the yellow triangle squares.

4. Sew the remaining 32 units from Step 1 into pairs to make 16 half-circle units **(fig. 6)**. Press all seams open.

5. Sew the units made in Step 3 and Step 4 together in the orientation shown **(fig. 6)** for a total of 16 petal blocks. Press seams open.

6. Sew a black 1¾" × 1¾" (4.5 × 4.5cm) square along the diagonal to each petal block in the bottom right-hand corner curve in the orientation shown **(fig. 7)**. Flip and fold half of the square to align

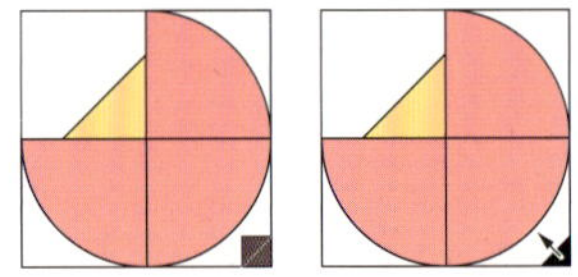

figure 7

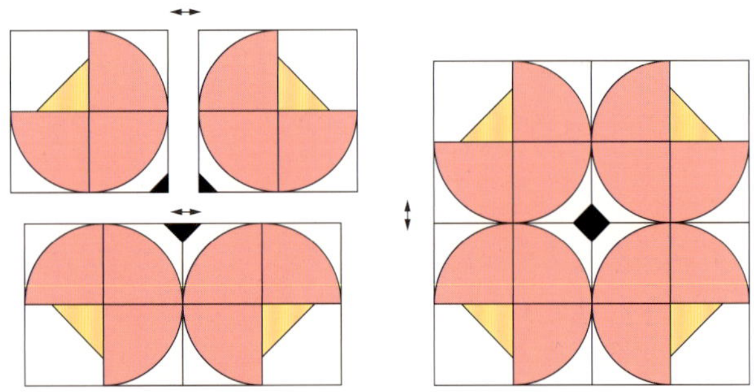

figure 8

with the edges of the block. Trim away the excess black and background fabric from the back of the quilt leaving a ¼" (6mm) seam allowance. Press the seam toward the background fabric. You will have a total of 16 petal blocks with a small black flip and fold corner.

7. Sew the petal blocks created in Step 6 together into pairs in the orientation shown, matching center and corner seams. Press the seams open. You will have a total of eight pairs of petal blocks **(fig. 8)**.

8. Sew each petal pair created in Step 7 to another in the orientation shown to create the flower blocks. Again, match center and corner seams and press the seams open. You will have a total of four flower blocks **(fig. 8)**.

MAKING THE QUILT TOP

Refer to the Full Bloom Construction Diagram for assembly of the quilt block units created in the previous section along with sashing and corner stones.

1. Sew three 22½" × 2½" (56 × 6.5cm) background sashing strips between four 2½" × 2½" (6.5 × 6.5cm) yellow cornerstone squares to make 4 sashing rows. Press seams toward the sashing.

2. Arrange the flower and leaf blocks in three rows of three blocks each, as shown in the Full Bloom Construction Diagram, alternating block orientation and inserting sashing as shown.

3. Sew the blocks with sashing together into rows, matching blocks and sashing edges. Press the seams toward the sashing.

4. Sew the rows together, matching sashing and corner stones. Press the seams toward the sashing.

FINISHING

1. Refer to Finishing your Quilt (page 122) or use your favorite methods to layer and baste the quilt top, batting, and backing.

2. Quilt as desired. Longarm quilter Melissa Snyder quilted my quilt with a flower and bud pantograph design I chose to mimic my quilt design of modern leaves and flowers.

3. Bind your quilt using my French double-fold binding method as described in Binding (page 126) or your own method as preferred.

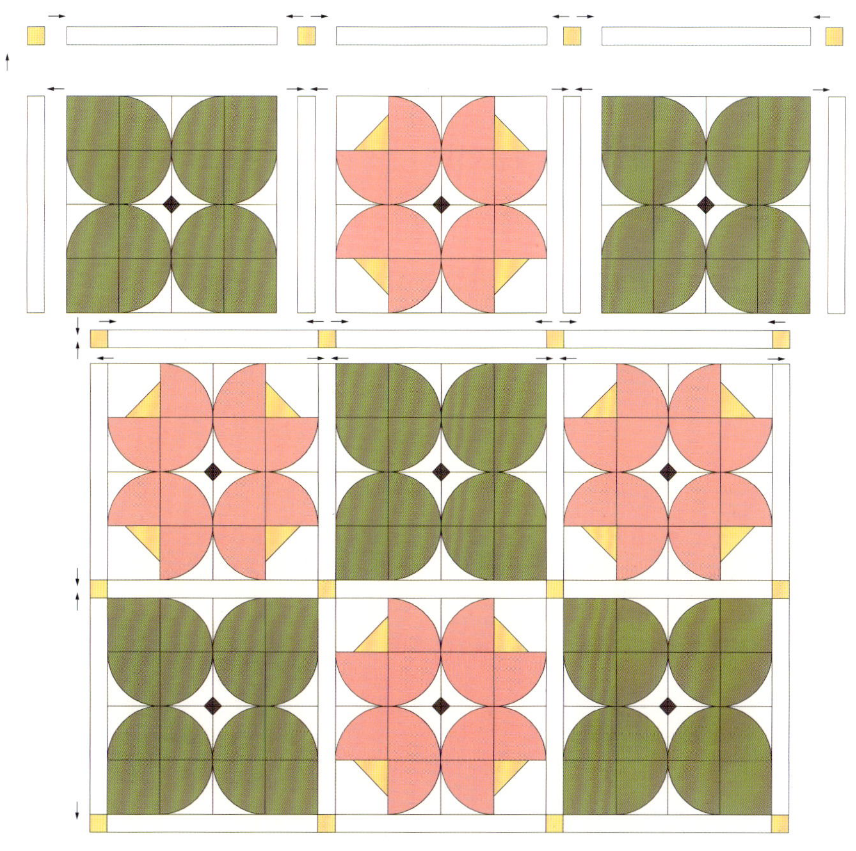

FULL BLOOM CONSTRUCTION DIAGRAM

BUTTERFLIES QUILT

Finished size: 60" × 84" (152.5 × 213cm)
Designed and pieced by Angela Pingel
Quilted by Krista Withers

I'm probably not supposed to have favorites, but I can't help it. This is my favorite quilt in the book. It is the perfect balance of function and whimsy. The curves are so charming in this quilt. I used them sparingly for optimum impact. Because this quilt has a large amount of negative space, the blocks come together quickly. And, with its organic nature and movement, this is an extremely forgiving pattern. Drop everything you are doing and make this one! I promise it is a quilt that will make you smile the whole time you are creating it.

MATERIALS

Fabric amounts are based on yardage with a usable width of 42" (106.5cm). Fat quarters are 18" × 22" (45.5 × 56cm).

5⅛ yd (4.7m) light blue print fabric

Note: Choose 1 medium and 1 dark value for each of the following fat quarters:

- 2 fat quarters orange print fabrics (orange #1 and #2)
- 2 fat quarters yellow print fabrics (yellow #1 and #2)
- 2 fat quarters purple print fabrics (purple #1 and #2)
- 2 fat quarters pink print fabrics (pink #1 and #2)

5¼ yd (4.8m) backing fabric

⅝ yd (57cm) binding fabric

68" × 92" (173 × 234cm) batting

TOOLS

Template patterns G and H (small); P and Q (medium); N and O (large)

Template plastic or paper

CUTTING

WOF = width of fabric

FROM LIGHT BLUE PRINT FABRIC:

- Cut 7 strips 12½" (31.5cm) × WOF. Cut 20 squares 12½" × 12½" (31.5 × 31.5cm) from the strips.
- Cut 5 strips 6½" (16.5cm) × WOF. Cut 27 squares 6½" × 6½" (16.5 × 16.5cm) from the strips.
- Cut 2 strips 6" (15cm) × WOF. Cut 12 squares 6" × 6" (15 × 15cm) from the strips. Cut 1 piece P from each square.
- Cut 1 strip 3½" (9cm) × WOF. Cut 11 squares 3½" × 3½" (9 × 9cm) from the strip.
- Cut 1 strip 5½" (14cm) × WOF. Cut 4 squares 5½" × 5½" (14 × 14cm) from the strip.
- Cut 4 strips 4½" (11.5cm) × WOF. Cut 33 squares 4½" × 4½" (11.5 × 11.5cm) from the strips. Cut 1 piece G from each square.

continued on next page

- Cut 2 strips 7½" (19cm) × WOF. Cut 6 squares 7½" × 7½" (19 × 19cm) from the strips. Cut 1 piece N from each square.
- Cut 3 strips 2½" (6.5cm) × WOF. Cut 2 pieces 2½" × 12½" (6.5 × 31.5cm) and 1 piece 2½" × 10½" (6.5 × 26.5cm) from 2 strips. Cut 2 pieces 2½" × 10½" (6.5 × 26.5cm) from remaining strip for a total of (4) 2½" × 12½" (6.5 × 31.5cm) and (4) 2½" × 10½" (6.5 × 26.5cm).

FROM ORANGE PRINT FAT QUARTER #1 (BUTTERFLY BODY):

- Cut 1 strip 5½" × 22" (14 × 56cm). Cut 2 squares 5½" × 5½" (14 × 14cm) from the strip. Cut 1 piece Q from each square.
- Cut 1 strip 3½" × 22" (9 × 56cm). Cut 2 squares 3½" × 3½" (9 × 9cm) from the strip. Cut 1 piece H from each square.

FROM ORANGE PRINT FAT QUARTER #2 (BUTTERFLY WINGS):

- Cut 2 strips 5½" × 22" (14 × 56cm). Cut 4 squares 5½" × 5½" (14 × 14cm) from the strips. Cut 1 piece Q from each square.
- Cut 1 strip 3½" × 22" (9 × 56cm). Cut 4 squares 3½" × 3½" (9 × 9cm) from the strip. Cut 1 piece H from each square.

FROM YELLOW PRINT FAT QUARTER #1 (BUTTERFLY BODY):

- Cut 1 strip 5½" × 22" (14 × 56cm). Cut 2 squares 5½" × 5½" (14 × 14cm) from the strip. Cut each square into 1 piece Q.
- Cut 1 strip 3½" × 22" (9 × 56cm). Cut 2 squares 3½" × 3½" (9 × 9cm) from the strip. Cut 1 piece H from each square.

FROM YELLOW PRINT FAT QUARTER #2 (BUTTERFLY WINGS):

- Cut 2 strips 5½" × 22" (14 × 56cm). Cut 4 squares 5½" × 5½" (14 × 14cm) from the strips. Cut 1 piece Q from each square.
- Cut 1 strip 3½" × 22" (9 × 56cm). Cut 4 squares 3½" × 3½" (9 × 9cm) from the strip. Cut 1 piece H from each square.

FROM PINK PRINT FAT QUARTER #1 (BUTTERFLY BODY):

- Cut 1 strip 3½" × 22" (9 × 56cm). Cut 2 squares 3½" × 3½" (9 × 9cm) from the strip. Cut 1 piece H from each square.
- Cut 1 strip 6½" × 22" (16.5 × 56cm). Cut 1 square 6½" × 6½" (16.5 × 16.5cm) from the strip. Cut 1 piece O from the square.

FROM PINK PRINT FAT QUARTER #2 (BUTTERFLY WINGS):

- Cut 1 strip 3½" × 22" (9 × 56cm). Cut 4 squares 3½" × 3½" (9 × 9cm) from the strip. Cut 1 piece H from each square.
- Cut 1 strip 6½" × 22" (16.5 × 56cm). Cut 2 squares 6½" × 6½" (16.5 × 16.5cm) from the strip. Cut 1 piece O from each strip.

FROM PURPLE PRINT FAT QUARTER #1 (BUTTERFLY BODY):

- Cut 1 strip 3½" × 22" (9 × 56cm). Cut 5 squares 3½" × 3½" (9 × 9cm) from the strip. Cut 1 piece H from each square.
- Cut 1 strip 6½" × 22" (16.5 × 56cm). Cut 1 square 6½" × 6½" (16.5 × 16.5cm) from the strip. Cut 1 piece O from the square.

FROM PURPLE PRINT FAT QUARTER #2 (BUTTERFLY WINGS):

- Cut 2 strips 3½" × 22" (9 × 56cm). Cut 10 squares 3½" × 3½" (9 × 9cm) from the strips. Cut 1 piece H from each square.
- Cut 1 strip 6½" × 22" (16.5 × 56cm). Cut 2 squares 6½" × 6½" (16.5 × 16.5cm) from the strip. Cut 1 piece O from each square.

FROM BACKING FABRIC:

- Cut 2 rectangles 92" (234cm) × WOF.

FROM BINDING FABRIC:

- Cut 8 strips 2½" (6.5cm) × WOF.

TIP

Are butterflies not your thing? You can easily accommodate the pattern to resemble other winged creatures. Try using a black fabric for the body and a red with black polka dot fabric for the wings to create a ladybug. Or use a yellow/black striped fabric for the body and yellow fabric for the wings to create a bumblebee. Appliquéd antennae create a more literal look for the creatures as well.

MAKING THE BLOCKS

Unfinished block size: 12½" x 12½" (31.5 x 31.5cm)
You will make butterfly units in three sizes for the blocks—eleven small, four medium, and two large. The small and medium butterfly units will be combined with the blue background pieces in different ways to form the full blocks. Each large butterfly unit is a complete block unto itself. The remaining blocks in the quilt are unpieced blue squares.

BASIC BUTTERFLY UNITS

Use the same basic method to make all three sizes of butterfly units. Begin by making quarter-circle unit pairs, then combine them to make butterfly units.

1. Sew together curved pieces G and H for the small butterflies **(fig. 1)** as follows:
   - Sew 2 blue print pieces G to 2 orange print #1 pieces H.
   - Sew 4 blue print pieces G to 4 orange print #2 pieces H.
   - Sew 2 blue print pieces G to 2 yellow print #1 pieces H.
   - Sew 4 blue print pieces G to 4 yellow print #2 pieces H.
   - Sew 2 blue print pieces G to 2 pink print #1 pieces H.
   - Sew 4 blue print pieces G to 4 pink print #2 pieces H.
   - Sew 5 blue print pieces G to 5 purple print #1 pieces H.
   - Sew 10 blue print pieces G to 10 purple print #2 pieces H.

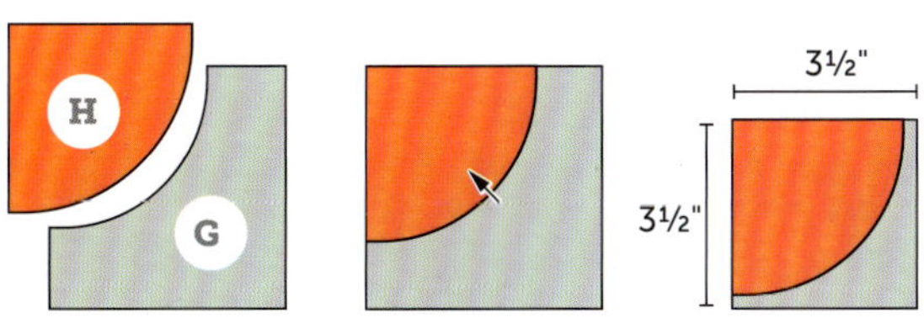

figure 1

   Press the seams toward piece H. Trim each unit to 3½" x 3½" (9 x 9cm) with a ¼" (6mm) seam allowance on piece G. You will have 33 small quarter-circle units.

2. Sew together curved pieces P and Q for the medium butterflies as follows:
   - Sew 2 blue print pieces P to 2 yellow print #1 pieces Q.
   - Sew 4 blue print pieces P to 4 yellow print #2 pieces Q.
   - Sew 2 blue print pieces P to 2 orange print #1 pieces Q.
   - Sew 4 blue print pieces P to 4 orange print #2 pieces Q.

   Press the seams toward piece Q. Trim each unit to 5½" x 5½" (14 x 14cm) with a ¼" (6mm) seam allowance on piece P. You will have 12 medium quarter-circle units.

3. Sew together curved pieces N and O for the large butterfly as follows:
   - Sew 1 blue print piece N to 1 pink print #1 piece O.
   - Sew 2 blue print pieces N to 2 pink print #2 pieces O.
   - Sew 1 blue print piece N to 1 purple print #1 piece O.
   - Sew 2 blue print pieces N to 2 purple print #2 pieces O.

   Press the seams toward piece O. Trim each unit to 6½" x 6½" (16.5 x 16.5cm) with a ¼" (6mm) seam allowance on piece N. You will have six large quarter-circle units.

4. Refer to **Figure 2** and **Figure 3** to assemble the small butterfly units. Sew a blue print square 3½" x 3½" (9 x 9cm) to one wing unit. Press the seam toward the blue print square. Sew the remaining wing unit to the body unit. Press the seam toward the wing fabrics. Sew the two pieces together, matching the center seams. Press the seam open. Make a total of 11 small butterfly units.

5. Refer to **Figure 2** and **Figure 3** to assemble the medium butterfly units. Sew a blue print square 5½" x 5½" (14 x 14cm) to one wing unit. Press the seam toward the blue print square. Sew the remaining wing unit to the body unit. Press the seam toward the wing fabrics. Sew the two pieces together, matching the center seams. Press the seam open. Make a total of four medium butterfly units.

6. Refer to **Figure 2** and **Figure 3** to assemble the large butterfly blocks. Sew a blue print square 6½" x 6½" (16.5 x 16.5cm) to one wing unit. Press the seam toward the blue print square. Sew the remaining wing unit to the body unit. Press the seam toward the wing fabrics. Sew the two pieces together, matching the center seams. Press the seam open. Make a total of two large butterfly blocks.

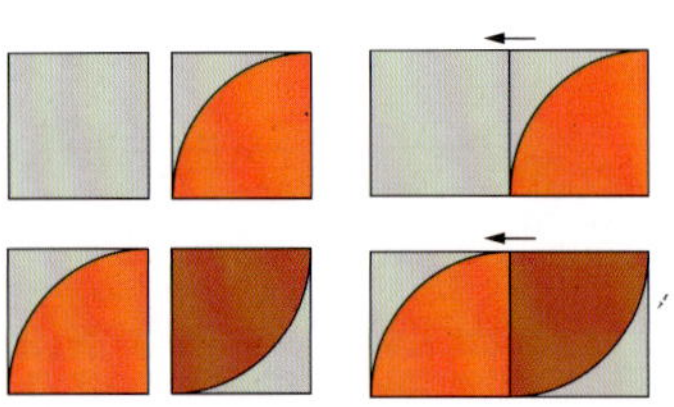

figure 2

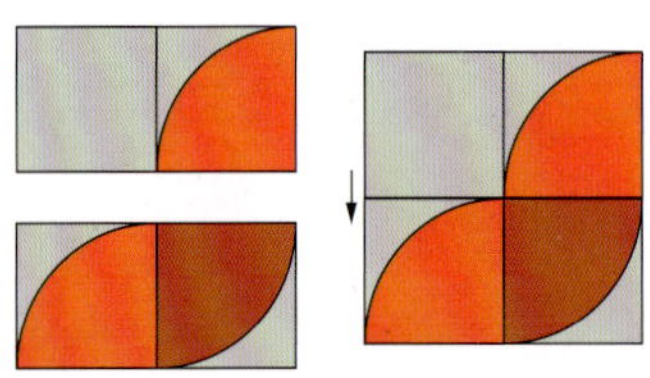

figure 3

SMALL BUTTERFLY BLOCKS

Refer to the Butterflies Construction Diagram (page 93) to correctly orient placement of the butterflies. There are four variations of the block made with small butterflies.

1. For Small Butterfly Block #1, make two blocks with purple print butterflies and one with an orange print butterfly. For each block, sew together two blue print squares 3½" x 3½" (9 x 9cm). Press the seam to the right. Sew a blue print square 3½" x 3½" (9 x 9cm) to a small butterfly unit. Press the seam to the left. Sew together the top and bottom units, matching center seams **(fig. 4)**. Press the seam open.

2. For Small Butterfly Block #2, make three blocks with purple print butterflies. For each block, sew a small butterfly unit to a blue square 6½" x 6½" (16.5 x 16.5cm). Press the seam to the right. Sew together two blue print squares 6½" x 6½" (16.5 x 16.5cm). Press the seam to the left. Sew together the top and bottom units, matching center seams **(fig. 5)**. Press the seam open.

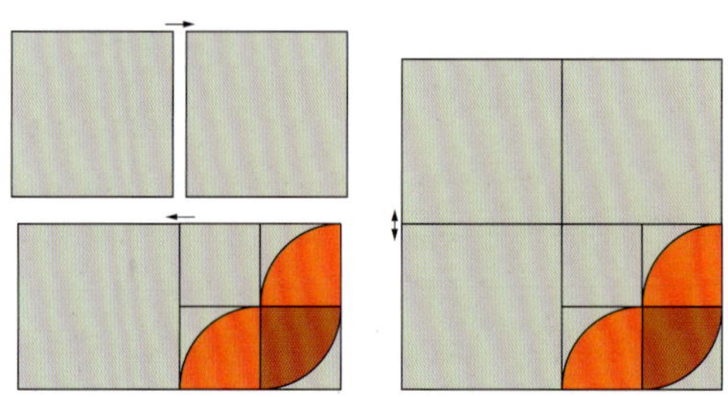

figure 4

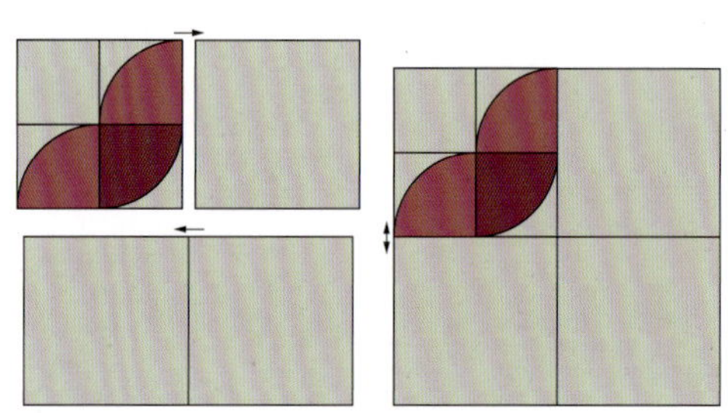

figure 5

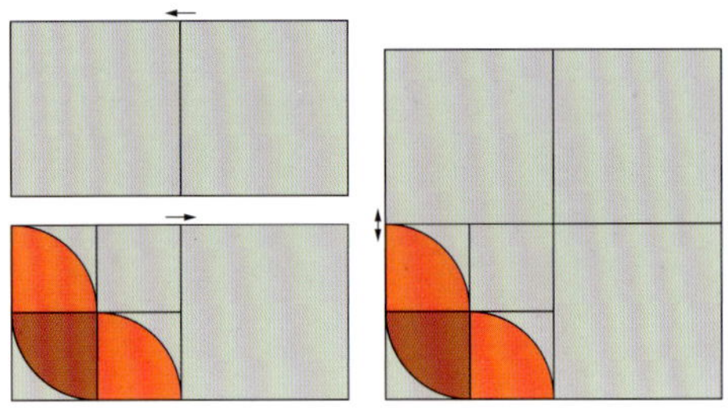

figure 6

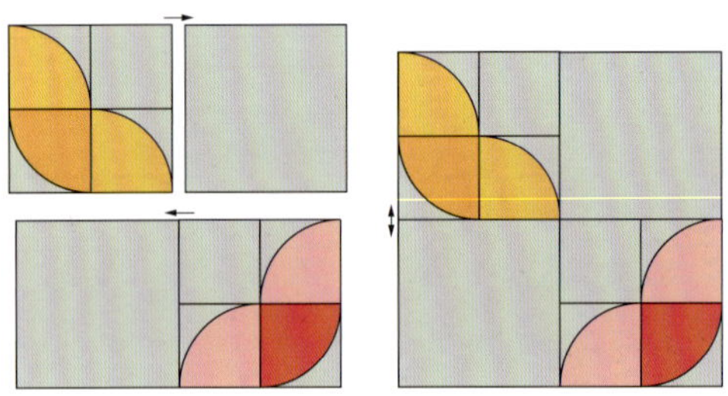

figure 7

3. For Small Butterfly Block #3, make one block with an orange print butterfly. Sew together two blue print squares 6½" × 6½" (16.5 × 16.5cm). Press the seam to the left. Sew a small butterfly unit to a blue print square 6½" × 6½" (16.5 × 16.5cm). Press the seam to the right. Sew together the top and bottom units, matching center seams **(fig. 6)**. Press the seam open.

4. For Small Butterfly Block #4, make two blocks with one yellow print butterfly and one pink print butterfly. For each block, sew a small butterfly unit to a blue square 6½" × 6½" (16.5 × 16.5cm). Press the seam to the right. Sew a blue print square 6½" × 6½" (16.5 × 16.5cm) to a small butterfly block. Press the seam to the left. Sew together the top and bottom units, matching center seams **(fig. 7)**. Press the seam open.

MEDIUM BUTTERFLY BLOCKS

Make four blocks.

1. For each block, sew a blue print strip 2½" × 10½" (6.5 × 26.5cm) to the top of a PQ block with fabric #1 in the bottom right corner **(fig. 8)**. Press the seam toward the strip.

2. Sew a blue print strip 2½" × 12½" (6.5 × 31.5cm) to the left side **(fig. 9)**. Press the seam toward the strip. You will have two yellow print and two orange print blocks.

MAKING THE QUILT TOP

1. Refer to the Butterflies Construction Diagram to lay out seven rows of five blocks each. Use the small, medium, and large butterfly blocks along with the 20 blue squares 12½" × 12½" (31.5 × 31.5cm). Note the block size, color, and orientation.

2. Sew the blocks into rows as shown. Press the seams in one direction, alternating for adjacent rows.

3. Sew the rows together to make the quilt top. Press seams in one direction.

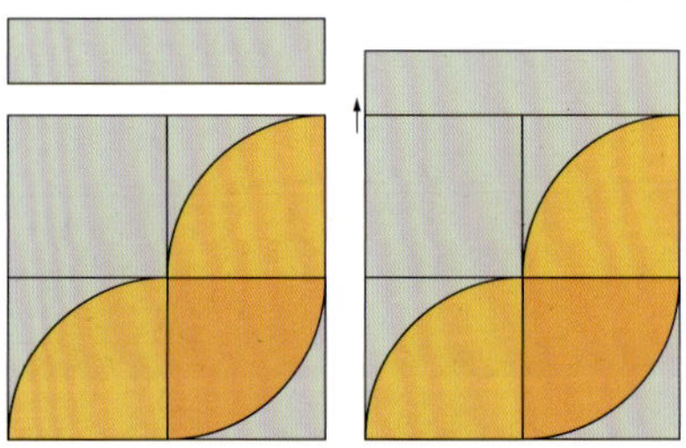

figure 8

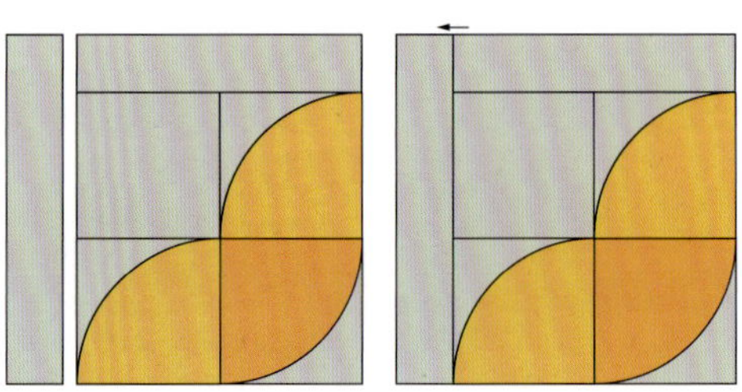

figure 9

FINISHING

1. Refer to Finishing Your Quilt (page 122) or use your favorite methods to layer and baste the quilt top, batting, and backing.

2. Quilt as desired. Longarm quilter Krista Withers shows off her talent with her creative quilting. She added swirling gusts of wind, straight-line sections, and detailed quilting on each butterfly.

3. Bind your quilt using my French double fold binding method as described in Binding (page 126) or your own preferred method.

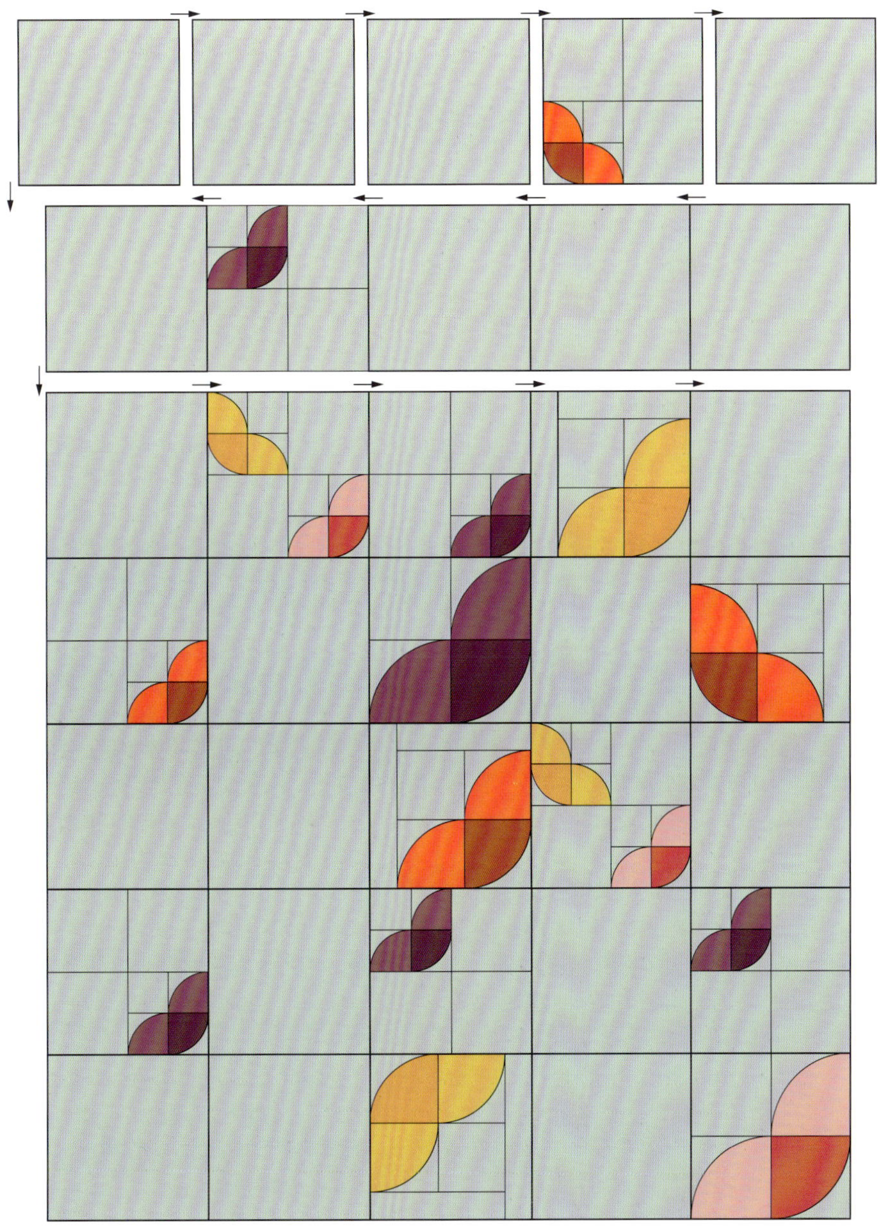

BUTTERFLIES CONSTRUCTION DIAGRAM

BRIGHT IDEAS WALL HANGING

Finished size: 25" × 35½" (63.5 × 90cm)
Designed, pieced, and quilted by Angela Pingel

This trio of pencils is the perfect addition for a teacher's classroom, a nursery, or really anywhere you use pencils. With just a hint of curved piecing, the Bright Ideas Wall Hanging is a perfect beginner project. And it is just seriously adorable. Whether you use some scrappy print fabrics as I did here or grab some gold #2 solid pencils look-alike fabric, you can create the perfect box of tools that will inspire all who value the humble pencil.

MATERIALS

Fabric amounts are based on yardage with a usable width of 42" (106.5cm).

½ yd (45.5cm) background fabric

1 fat quarter (46 × 56cm) light pink print fabric

1 fat quarter (46 × 56cm) dark pink print fabric

1 fat quarter (46 × 56cm) light aqua print fabric

1 fat quarter (46 × 56cm) dark aqua print fabric

1 fat quarter (46 × 56cm) light yellow print fabric

1 fat quarter (46 × 56cm) dark yellow print fabric

1 fat quarter (46 × 56cm) tan solid fabric

3 rectangles 2" × 6½" (5 × 17cm) black print fabric

1 yd (91cm) backing fabric

¼ yd (23cm) binding fabric

28" × 38" (71 × 97cm) batting

TOOLS

Template patterns R, S, T, U, V, W, G, and H

Template plastic or paper

CUTTING

WOF = width of fabric

FROM BACKGROUND FABRIC:

- Cut 3 strips 2½" (6.5cm) × WOF.
  - Subcut 2 strips 2½" × 30" (6.5 × 76cm) for a total of two 2½" × 30" (6.5 × 76cm) strips.
  - Subcut 1 strip 2½" × 25" (6.5 × 63.5cm) and discard remaining strip fabric.
- Cut 2 strips 2" (5cm) × WOF.
  - Subcut 2 strips 2" × 30" (5 × 76cm).
- Cut 1 strip 4½" (11.5cm) × WOF.
  - Subcut 1 strip 4½" × 25" (11.5 × 63.5cm).
- Cut 1 strip 8" (20cm) × WOF.
  - Subcut 3 squares 8" × 8" (20 × 20cm). Cut 1 piece V and 1 piece W from each square for a total of 3 pieces V and 3 pieces W.
- Cut 1 strip 3½" (9cm) × WOF.
  - Subcut 6 squares 3½" × 3½" (9 × 9cm). Cut 6 pieces G from the squares.

continued on next page

FROM LIGHT PINK PRINT FABRIC:

- Cut 1 strip 3½" × 18½" (9 × 47cm).
- Cut 2 squares 3½" 3½" (9 × 9cm). Cut 1 piece H from each square for a total of 2 pieces H.
- Cut 1 square 3" × 3" (8 × 8cm). Cut 1 piece U from the square.
- Cut 1 square 2½" × 2½" (6.5 × 6.5cm). Cut 2 pieces S from the square.

FROM DARK PINK PRINT FABRIC:

- Cut 2 strips 2" × 18½" (5 × 47cm).
- Cut 1 square 2½" × 2½" (6.5 × 6.5cm). Cut 2 pieces S from the square.

FROM LIGHT AQUA PRINT FABRIC:

- Cut 1 strip 3½" × 18½" (9 × 47cm).
- Cut 2 squares 3½" 3½" (9 × 9cm). Cut 1 piece H from each square for a total of 2 pieces H.
- Cut 1 square 3" × 3" (8 × 8cm). Cut 1 piece U from the square.
- Cut 1 square 2½" × 2½" (6.5 × 6.5cm). Cut 2 pieces S from the square.

FROM DARK AQUA PRINT FABRIC:

- Cut 2 strips 2" × 18½" (5 × 47cm).
- Cut 1 square 2½" × 2½" (6.5 × 6.5cm). Cut 2 pieces S from the square.

FROM LIGHT YELLOW PRINT FABRIC:

- Cut 1 strip 3½" × 18½" (9 × 47cm).
- Cut 2 squares 3½" 3½" (9 × 9cm). Cut 1 piece H from each square for a total of 2 pieces H.
- Cut 1 square 3" × 3" (8 × 8cm). Cut 1 piece U from the square.
- Cut 1 square 2½" × 2½" (6.5 × 6.5cm). Cut 2 pieces S from the square.

FROM DARK YELLOW PRINT FABRIC:

- Cut 2 strips 2" × 18½" (5 × 47cm).
- Cut 1 square 2½" × 2½" (6.5 × 6.5cm). Cut 2 pieces S from the square.

FROM TAN SOLID FABRIC:

- Cut 3 strips 4½" × 7" (11.5 × 18cm). Cut 1 piece T from each strip for a total of 3 CC pieces.
- Cut 6 strips 2½" × 3½" (6.5 × 9cm). Cut 1 piece R from each strip for a total of 6 pieces R.

FROM BLACK PRINT FABRIC:

- Cut 3 rectangles 2" × 6½" (5 × 17cm).

FROM BACKING FABRIC:

- Cut 1 piece 29" × 39" (74 × 99cm).

FROM BINDING FABRIC:

- Cut 4 strips 2¼" (6cm) × WOF.

TIP

Part of the fun of this design is making the wall hanging super scrappy by using multiple fabrics. While I would suggest keeping the shaved pencil color uniform between the three pencils (I used a tan solid fabric), follow my version shown to see where you can mix and match the pencil tips, erasers, and metal band. Each piece can be made from a small scrap, so it is a great place to use that last precious piece of fabric from your favorite designer.

MAKING THE PENCILS

Unfinished block size: 6½" x 30" (16.5 x 76cm) This wall hanging has three pencil blocks.

1. Sew each print piece H to background piece G. Press the seams toward piece H. Trim each unit to 3½" x 3½" (9 x 9cm) leaving a ¼" (6mm) seam allowance on the G piece **(fig. 1)**. You will have a total of two quarter circle GH units with light pink print H, two quarter-circle GH units with light aqua print and two quarter-circle units GH with light yellow print. Arrange into pairs by color.

2. Sew the units from Step 1 into pairs to make three half-circle units **(fig. 2)**. Press all seams open.

3. Sew a black print rectangle 2" x 6½" (5 x 17cm) to the top of each half-circle unit made in Step 2 along the 6½" (17cm) edge **(fig. 3)**. Press seams toward the black print fabric. This creates the eraser blocks.

4. Sew a dark aqua print rectangle 2" x 18½" (5 x 47cm) to either side of the light aqua print rectangle 3½" x 18½" (9 x 47cm) along the 18½" (47cm) edge. Press seams toward the dark print fabric. Repeat for the pink print and yellow print fabrics to create three rectangle strip sets, one in aqua, one in pink and one in yellow **(fig. 4)**. This creates the pencil body blocks.

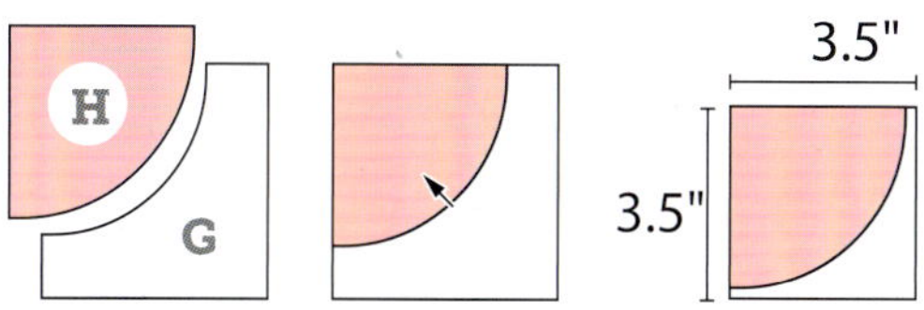

figure 1

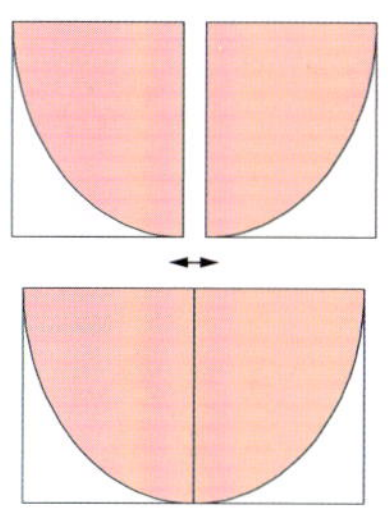

figure 2

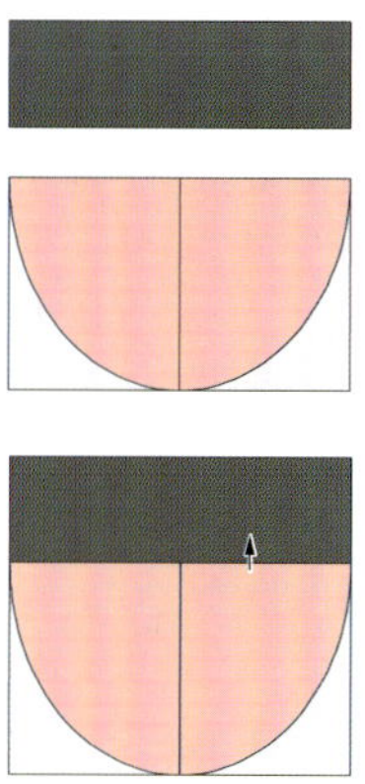

figure 3

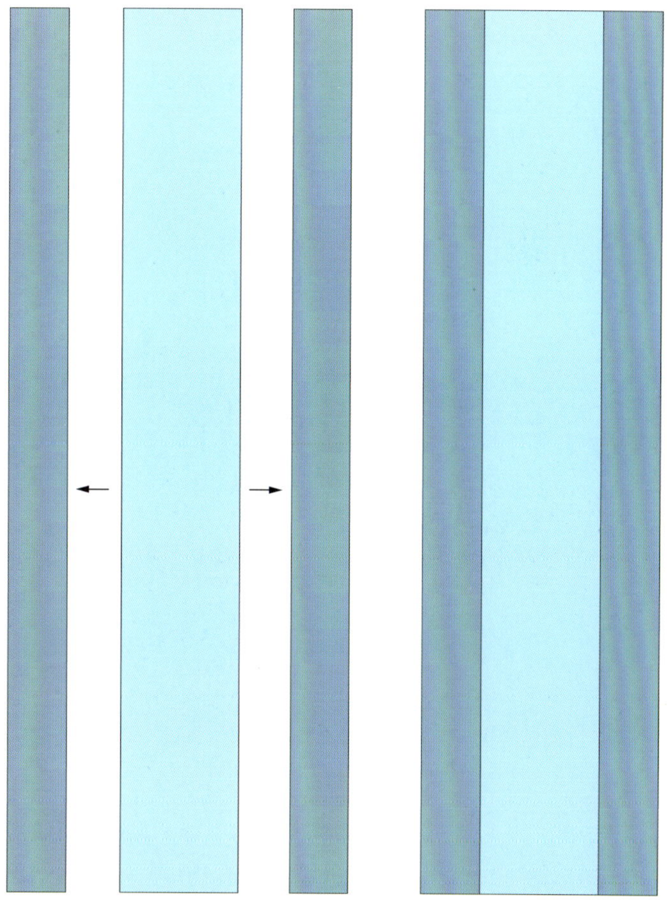

figure 4

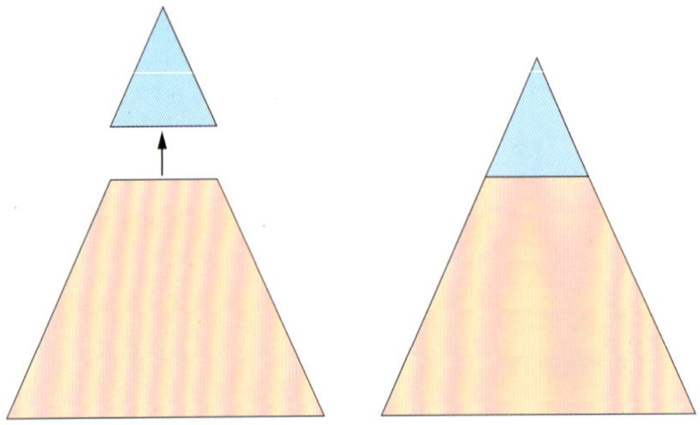

figure 5

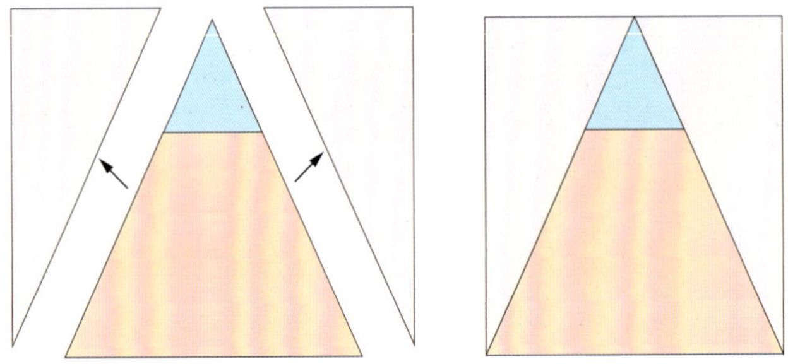

figure 6

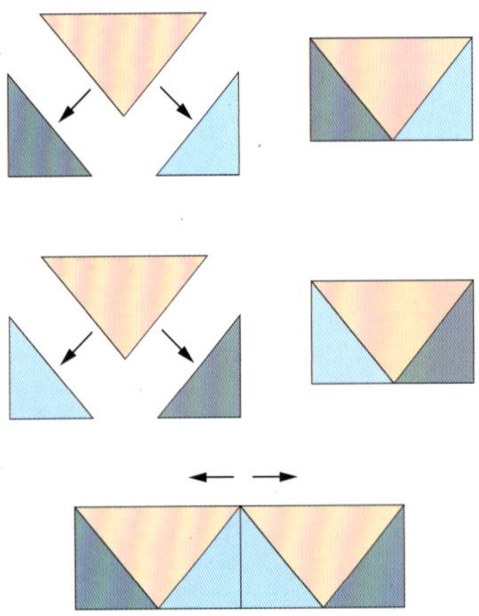

figure 7

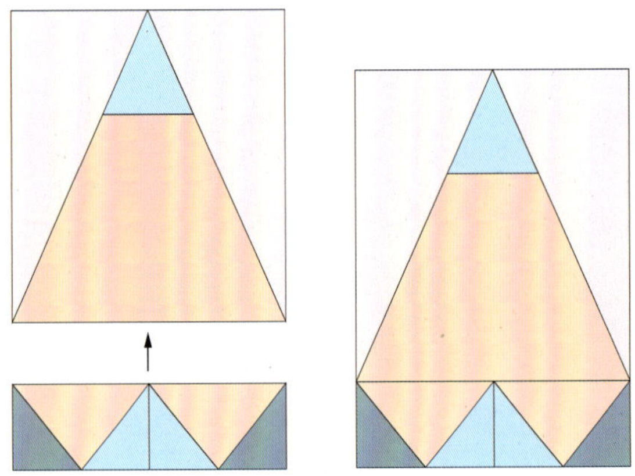

figure 8

5. Sew a light aqua print piece U to tan solid T piece along the 2½" (6.5cm) edge. Press seam toward the U piece. Repeat for the pink print and yellow print fabrics to create three pencil tip sets, one in aqua, one in pink, and one in yellow **(fig. 5)**.

6. Sew pieces V and W to either side of the piece made in step 5 along the long diagonal edges. Press seams toward the background fabric. Repeat for the pink print and yellow print fabrics to create three pencil tip blocks, one in aqua, one in pink, and one in yellow **(fig. 6)**.

7. Sew a dark aqua print and a light aqua print piece S to either side of a tan solid R piece along the diagonal in the orientation shown **(fig. 7)**. Reverse the color orientation and sew a second set of three triangles together. Press all seams toward the aqua print fabrics.

   Sew the two aqua print triangle blocks together with light aqua print fabrics adjoining the 2" (5cm) edges. This creates the appearance of a complete light aqua print triangle and two dark aqua print half triangles. Repeat for the pink print and yellow print fabrics to create three pencil carving blocks, one in aqua, one in pink, and one in yellow.

8. Sew together the aqua pencil tip block created in step 6 to the aqua pencil carving block created in step 7 in the orientation shown along the 6½" (16.5cm) edge **(fig. 8)**. Press the seams toward the pencil tip block. This creates the upper pencil block. Repeat for the pink print and yellow print fabrics to create three upper pencil blocks, one in aqua, one in pink, and one in yellow.

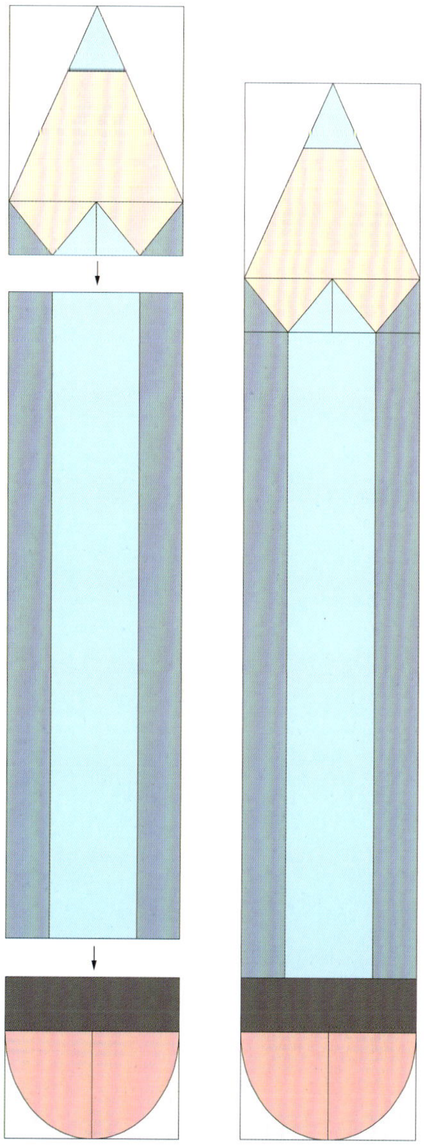

figure 9

9. Sew together the aqua upper pencil block to the aqua pencil body block to the pink eraser block along the 6½" (16.5cm) edges as shown **(fig. 9)**. Press all seams down toward the eraser block. Repeat for the pink print pencil body block to the yellow eraser block and the yellow print pencil body block to the aqua eraser block to create three pencil blocks, one in aqua/pink, one in pink/yellow and one in yellow/aqua.

MAKING THE WALL HANGING TOP

1. Arrange the pencil blocks in a row as shown in the Bright Ideas Construction Diagram, in block orientation as shown. Laid out from left to right is the aqua pencil followed by the yellow pencil, and then the pink pencil. Sew a background fabric strip 2" × 30" (5 × 76cm) between each pencil block along the 30" (76cm) edges. Press seams toward the background strips.

BRIGHT IDEAS CONSTRUCTION DIAGRAM

2. Sew the background fabric strips 2½" × 30" (6.5 × 76cm) on either side of the pencil row along the 30" (76cm) edges. Press seams toward the background strips.

3. Sew a background fabric strip 2½" × 25" (6.5 × 63.5cm) below the pencil row along the 25" (63.5cm) edges. Press seam towards the background strip.

4. Sew a background fabric strip 4½" × 25" (11.5 × 63.5cm) above the pencil row along the 25" (63.5cm) edges. Press seam towards the background strip.

FINISHING

1. Refer to Finishing your Quilt (page 122) or use your favorite methods to layer and baste the quilt top, batting, and backing.

2. Quilt as desired. I quilted the wall hanging with diagonal crisscross straight lines to mimic the lines that a sharp pencil makes.

3. Bind your quilt using my French double-fold binding method as described in Binding (page 126) or your own method as preferred.

ORNAMENTAL QUILT

Finished size: 68" × 84" (173 × 213cm)
Designed and pieced by Angela Pingel
Quilted by Krista Withers

This quilt is designed to use those special charm squares of fabric you've been hoarding. Showcase your favorite fabrics in a minimalist, but never boring, design of curves. A background of solid or solid-like fabric contrasts well with the colors of the charms. Monochromatic fabrics or tone-on-tone fabrics best show the beautiful curves of the ornament motifs.

MATERIALS

Fabric amounts are based on yardage with a usable width of 42" (106.5cm). A charm square is 5" × 5" (12.5 × 12.5cm).

12 assorted fuchsia charm squares

12 assorted aqua charm squares

12 assorted red charm squares

10 assorted green charm squares

10 assorted yellow charm squares

5½ yd (5m) black linen fabric

5¼ yd (4.8m) backing fabric

⅔ yd (61cm) binding fabric

76" × 92" (193 × 234cm) batting

TOOLS

Template patterns E and F for the large units, and L and M for the small units

Template plastic or paper

CUTTING

WOF = width of fabric

FROM FUCHSIA CHARM SQUARES:

- From each of 4 squares, cut 1 piece E. From each of 4 squares, cut 1 piece F.

FROM AQUA CHARM SQUARES:

- From each of 4 squares, cut 1 piece E. From each of 4 squares, cut 1 piece F.

FROM RED CHARM SQUARES:

- From each of 4 squares, cut 1 piece E. From each of 4 squares, cut 1 piece F.

FROM GREEN CHARM SQUARES:

- Cut a square 4½" × 4½" (11.5 × 11.5cm) from each of 10 charm squares. From each of 4 squares, cut 1 piece L. From each of 4 squares, cut 1 piece M.

FROM YELLOW CHARM SQUARES:

- Cut a square 4½" × 4½" (11.5 × 11.5cm) from each of 10 charm squares. From each of 4 squares, cut 1 piece L. From each of 4 squares, cut 1 piece M.

continued on next page

FROM BLACK LINEN FABRIC:

- Cut 8 strips 16½" (42cm) × WOF. From the strips, cut 15 squares 16½" × 16½" (42 × 42cm).
- Cut 4 strips 5" (12.5cm) × WOF. From the strips, cut 32 squares 5" × 5" (12.5 × 12.5cm). From the squares, cut 20 pieces E and 12 pieces F.
- Cut 3 strips 4½" (11.5cm) × WOF. Cut the strips into 20 squares 4½" × 4½" (11.5 × 11.5cm).
- Cut 11 strips 2½" (6.5cm) × WOF.
  - From 2 strips, cut 4 strips 2½" × 16½" (6.5 × 42cm).
  - From 1 strip, cut 4 rectangles 2½" × 4½" (6.5 × 11.5cm) and 8 squares 2½" × 2½" (6.5 × 6.5cm). Cut 1 piece M from each square.
- Use the remaining 8 strips for the borders.

FROM BACKING FABRIC:

- Cut 2 rectangles 92" (234cm) × WOF.

FROM BINDING FABRIC:

- Cut 8 strips 2½" (6.5cm) × WOF.

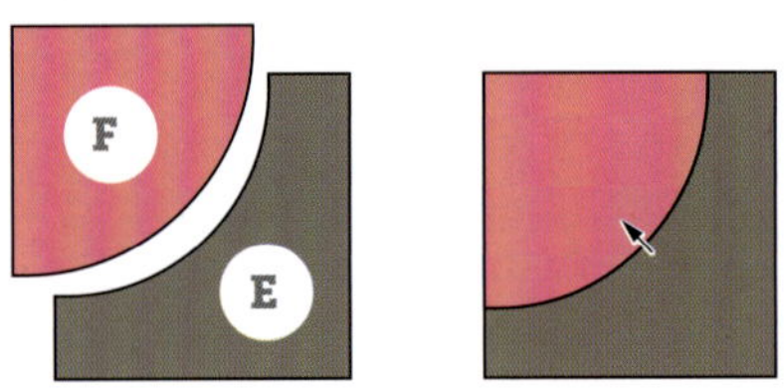

figure 1

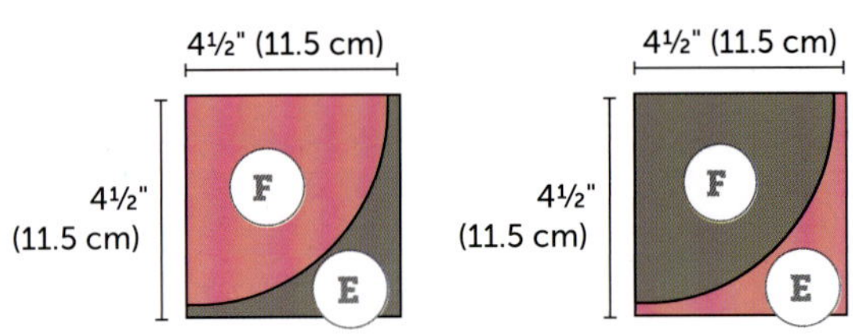

figure 2

MAKING THE BLOCKS

This quilt has three large and two small orb blocks.

LARGE ORB BLOCKS

Unfinished block size: 16½" × 16½" (42 × 42cm)
Make three blocks, one each of fuchsia, red, and aqua.

1. Sew together curved pieces E and F **(fig. 1)**. Sew four black linen pieces E to four fuchsia pieces F. Sew four fuchsia pieces E to four black linen pieces F. Press the seams toward piece F. Trim the unit to 4½" × 4½" (11.5 × 11.5cm), leaving a ¼" (6mm) seam allowance on G **(fig. 2)**. You will have a total of eight fuchsia/black quarter-circle units.

2. Repeat Step 1 to make eight quarter-circle units in red/ black and eight units in aqua/black.

3. Assemble each of the three blocks in four rows of four units **(fig. 3)**. Use four black linen squares 4½" × 4½" (11.5 × 11.5cm), four colored squares 4½" × 4½" (11.5 × 11.5cm), and the eight quarter-circle units. Press all seams open.

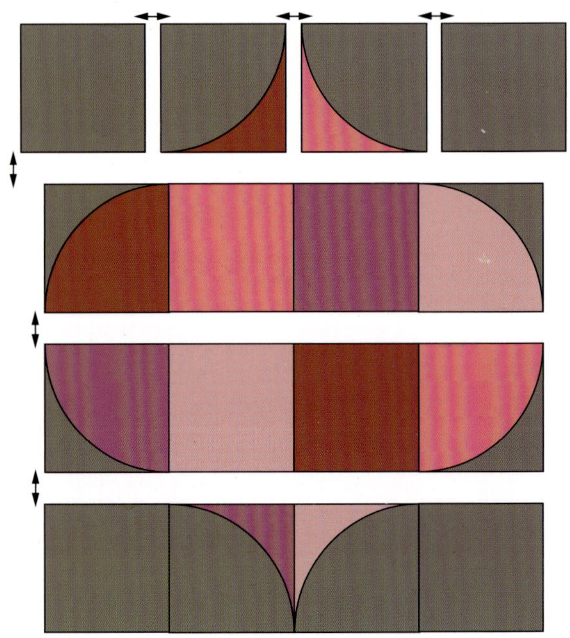

figure 3

SMALL ORB BLOCKS

Unfinished block size: 16½" × 16½" (42 × 42cm)
Make two blocks, one each of green and yellow.

1. Sew together curved pieces L and M **(fig. 4)**. Sew four black linen pieces M to four green pieces L. Press the seams toward piece M. Trim the LM units to 2½" × 2½" (6.5 × 6.5cm), leaving a ¼" (6mm) seam allowance on piece L **(fig. 5)**. You will have a total of four green/black small quarter-circle units. Repeat to make four yellow/black small quarter-circle units. Repeat to make four sets each of black/green and black/yellow EF units, trimming those to 4½" × 4½" (11.5 × 11.5cm).

2. Sew two sets of LM quarter-circle units together as shown **(fig. 6)**. Press the seams open. Sew one black linen rectangle 2½" × 4½" (6.5 × 11.5cm) to the long edge of each completed unit, noting the unit orientation. Press the seam toward the black linen rectangle. Sew one black linen square 4½" × 4½" (11.5 × 11.5cm) to either end of each piece. Press the seams open.

3. Sew one LM quarter-circle unit to either side of each 4½" × 4½" (11.5 × 11.5cm) colored print square, noting the orientation of the curves **(fig. 7)**. Press the seams open.

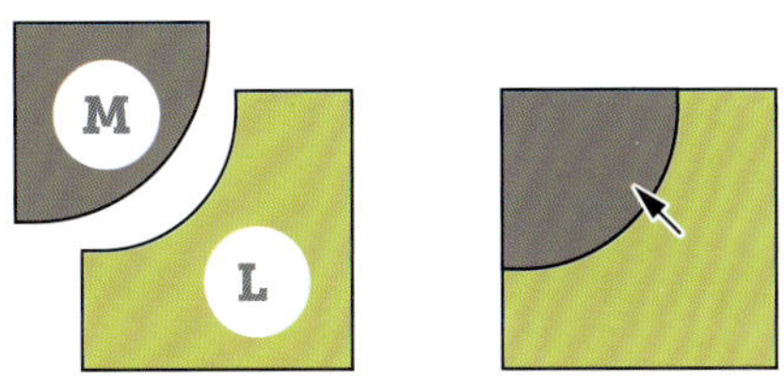

figure 4

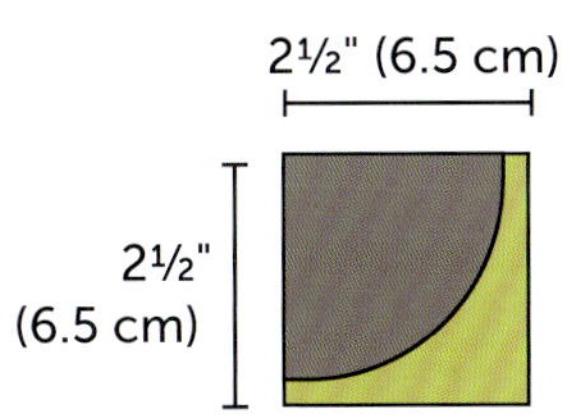

figure 5

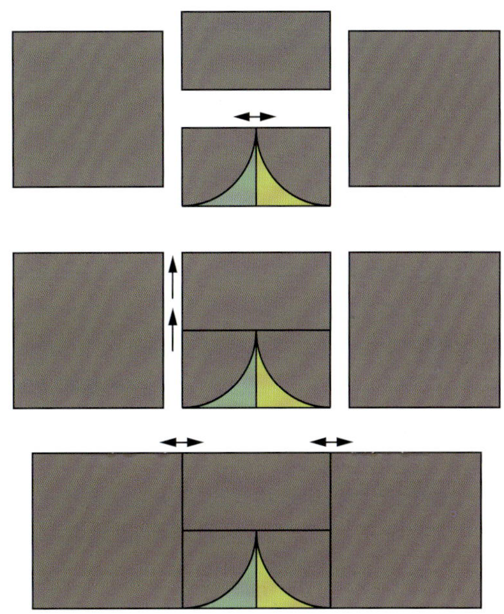

figure 6

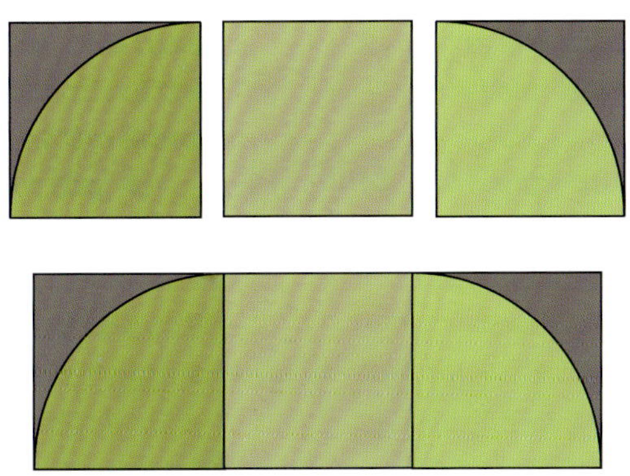

figure 7

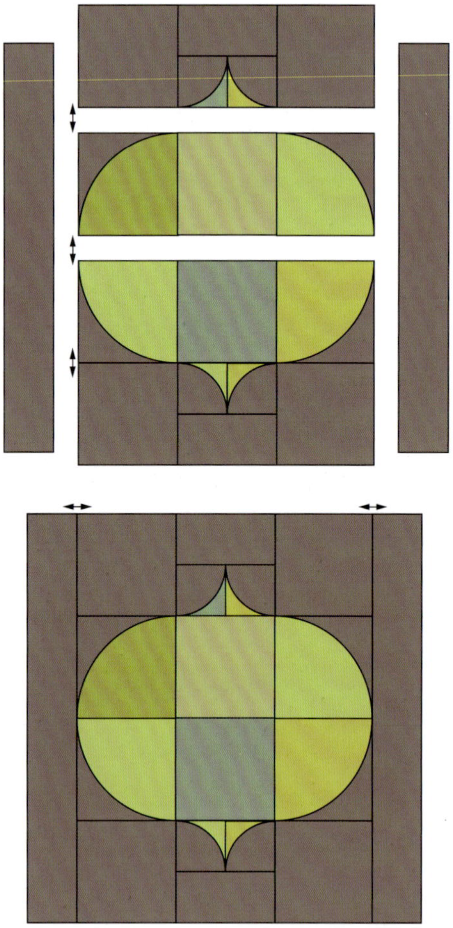

figure 8

4. Sew the four completed rows together in order, matching adjacent seams **(fig. 8)**. Press the seams open. Sew one black linen strip 2½" × 16½" (6.5 × 42cm) to either side of the block center. Press the seams toward the black linen fabric.

MAKING THE QUILT TOP

1. Lay out the 15 black linen blocks 16½" × 16½" (42 × 42cm) and the large and small pieced orb blocks in five rows of four blocks each, as shown in the Ornamental Construction Diagram. Sew the blocks into rows. Press the seams in one direction, alternating by row. Sew together the rows matching adjacent seams. Press the seams open.

2. For the side borders, sew together two black linen strips 2½" (6.5cm) × WOF, and trim to 2½" × 80½" (6.5 × 204.5cm). Repeat to create a second strip.

3. For the top and bottom borders, sew together two black linen strips 2½" (6.5cm) × WOF, and trim to 2½" × 68½" (6.5 × 174cm). Repeat to create a second strip.

4. Sew one strip 2½" × 80½" (6.5 × 204.5cm) to each side of the quilt top. Press the seams toward the borders. Sew one strip 2½" × 68½" (6.5 × 174cm) to the quilt top and bottom. Press the seams toward the borders.

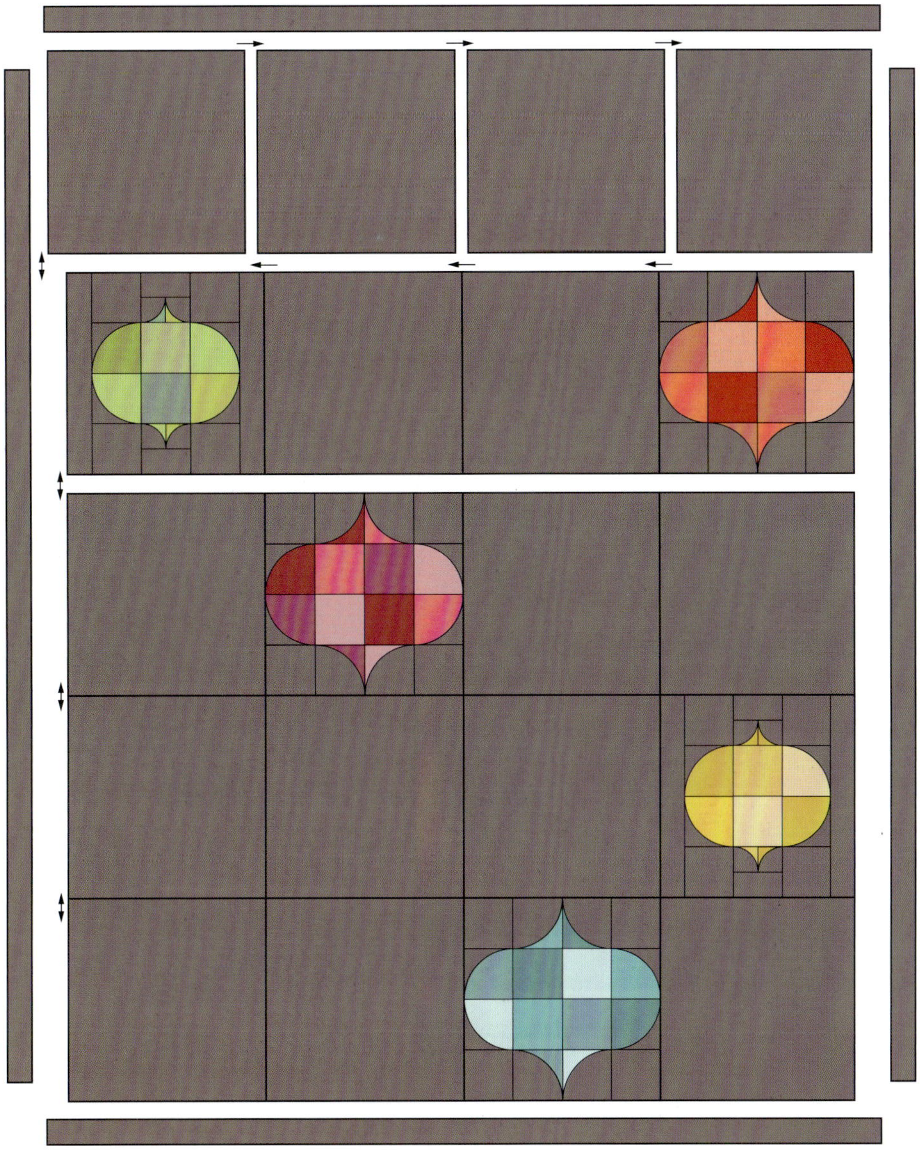

ORNAMENTAL CONSTRUCTION DIAGRAM

FINISHING

1. Refer to Finishing Your Quilt (page 122) or use your favorite methods to layer and baste the quilt top, batting, and backing.

2. Quilt as desired. Longarm quilter Krista Withers dressed up the large areas of negative space with a highly creative mixed pattern of bubbles, swirls, and spiral rectangles. Each ornament is treated to a complex quilting pattern reminiscent of antique ornaments for a Christmas tree.

3. Bind your quilt using my French double-fold binding method as described in Binding (page 126) or your own preferred method.

SUNRISE TABLE RUNNER

Finished Size: 16" × 40" (40.5 × 101.5cm)
Designed, pieced, and quilted by Angela Pingel

Color-blocked solids, interlocking curves, and dynamic back-and-forth movement make this runner a beautiful statement piece for your table. With colors reminiscent of a sunrise, and with curves running in all directions, dinner guests have an optimal view from wherever they're seated. Piece it with accuracy to create a truly seamless design. Moving in and out and up and down, this piece flows with the conversation.

MATERIALS

Fabric amounts are based on yardage with a usable width of 42" (106.5cm).

½ yd (45.5cm) blue solid fabric*

⅜ yd (34.5cm) yellow solid fabric

⅜ yd (34.5cm) orange solid fabric

⅝ yd (57cm) pink solid fabric

⅝ yd (57cm) purple solid fabric

1¼ yd (114.5cm) backing fabric

½ yd (45.5cm) diagonally printed stripe binding fabric

20" × 44" (51 × 112cm) batting

**I used a near-solid fabric.*

TOOLS

Template patterns E and F

Template plastic or paper

CUTTING

WOF = width of fabric

FROM BLUE SOLID FABRIC:

- Cut 2 strips 4½" (11.5cm) × WOF. Cut 12 squares 4½" × 4½" (11.5 × 11.5cm). Cut 1 piece F from each square.
- Cut 1 strip 5" (12.5cm) × WOF. Cut 8 squares 5" × 5" (12.5 × 12.5cm). Cut 1 piece E from each square.

FROM YELLOW SOLID FABRIC:

- Cut 1 strip 4½" (11.5cm) × WOF. Cut 4 squares 4½" × 4½" (11.5 × 11.5cm). Cut 1 piece F from each square.
- Cut 1 strip 5" (12.5cm) × WOF. Cut 6 squares 5" × 5" (12.5 × 12.5cm). Cut 1 piece E from each square.

FROM ORANGE SOLID FABRIC:

- Cut 1 strip 4½" (11.5cm) × WOF. Cut 4 squares 4½" × 4½" (11.5 × 11.5cm). Cut 1 piece F from each square.
- Cut 1 strip 5" (12.5cm) × WOF. Cut 6 squares 5" × 5" (12.5 × 12.5cm). Cut 1 piece E from each square.

continued on next page

FROM PINK SOLID FABRIC:

- Cut 2 strips 4½" (11.5cm) × WOF. Cut 10 squares 4½" × 4½" (11.5 × 11.5cm). Cut 1 piece F from each square.
- Cut 2 strips 5" × 5" (12.5 × 12.5cm) × WOF. Cut 10 squares 5" × 5" (12.5 × 12.5cm). Cut 1 piece E from each square.

FROM PURPLE SOLID FABRIC:

- Cut 2 strips 4½" (11.5cm) × WOF. Cut 10 squares 4½" × 4½" (11.5 × 11.5cm). Cut 1 piece F from each square.
- Cut 2 strips 5" (12.5cm) × WOF. Cut 10 squares 5" × 5" (12.5 × 12.5cm). Cut 1 piece E from each square.

FROM BACKING FABRIC:

- Cut 2 strips 20" (51cm) × WOF.

FROM BINDING FABRIC:

- Cut 3 strips 2½" (6.5cm) × WOF.

MAKING THE UNITS

Unfinished block size: 4½" × 4½" (11.5 × 11.5cm)
This runner has 40 quarter-circle units.
Sew together curved pieces E and F **(fig. 1)** as follows:

- Sew 6 yellow pieces E to 6 pink pieces F.
- Sew 6 orange pieces E to 6 purple pieces F.
- Sew 6 purple pieces E to 6 blue pieces F.
- Sew 6 pink pieces E to 6 blue pieces F.
- Sew 4 blue pieces E to 4 pink pieces F.
- Sew 4 blue pieces E to 4 purple pieces F.
- Sew 4 pink pieces E to 4 yellow pieces F.
- Sew 4 purple pieces E to 4 orange pieces F.

Press the seams toward piece F. Trim all blocks to 4½" × 4½" (11.5 × 11.5cm) with a ¼" (6mm) seam allowance on piece E. Make a total of 40 quarter-circle units.

MAKING THE RUNNER

The units for this runner are sewn into five sections.

1. Sections 1, 3, and 5 are identical. Each is composed of eight quarter-circle units. Refer to **Figure 2** for block color placement and orientation. Sew together the units for each section in pairs, and then sew the pairs together, carefully matching adjacent seams. Press all seams open. Make three sections.

2. Sections 2 and 4 are identical. Each is composed of eight quarter-circle units. Refer to **Figure 3** for block color placement and orientation. Sew together the units for each section in pairs, and then sew the pairs together, carefully matching adjacent seams. Press all seams open. Make two sections.

3. Refer to the Sunrise Table Runner Construction Diagram to sew together the table runner sections. First sew together sections 1 and 2. Continue to sew each section to another until complete, always matching adjacent seams. Press all seams open.

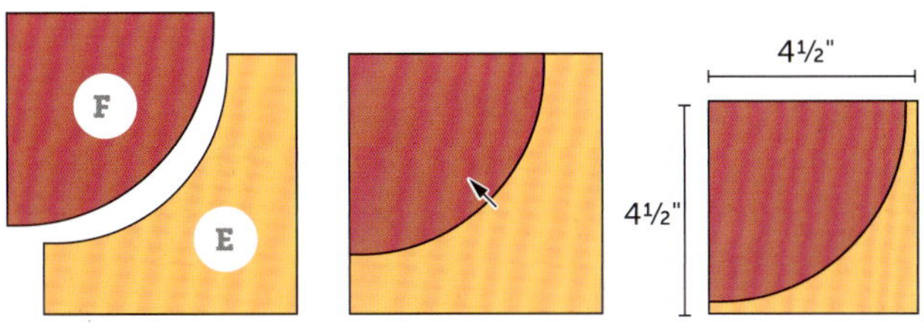

figure 1

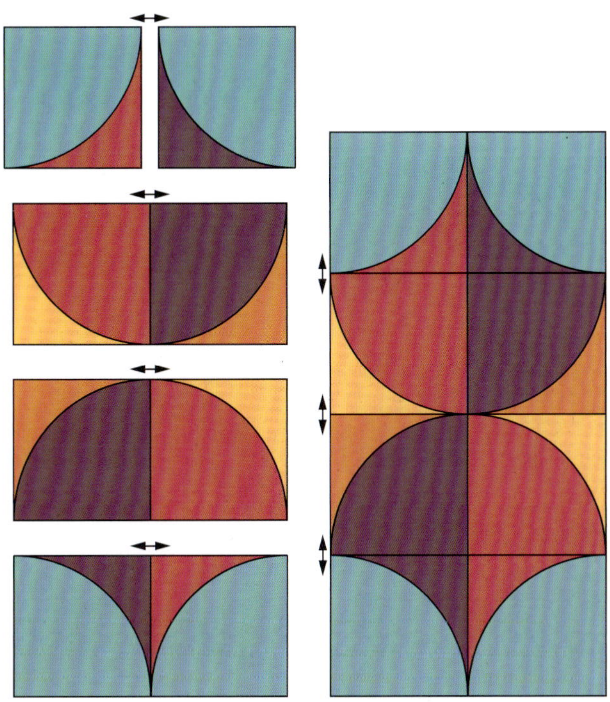

figure 2

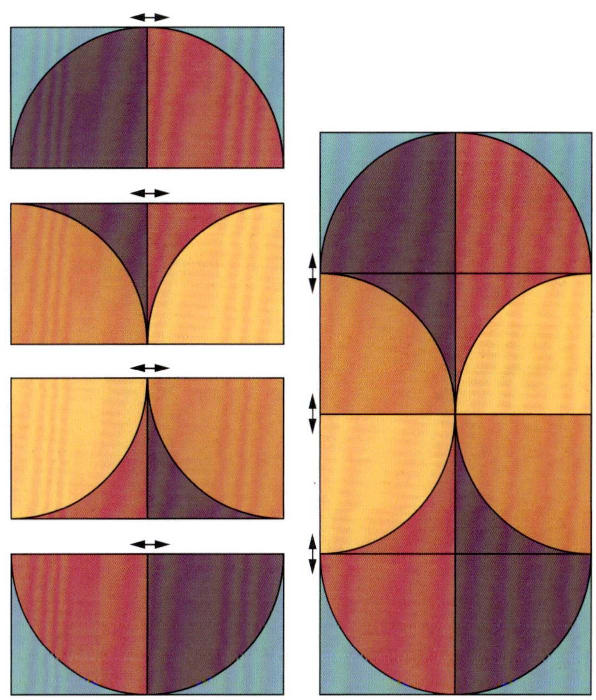

figure 3

SUNRISE TABLE RUNNER CONSTRUCTION DIAGRAM

FINISHING

1. Refer to Finishing Your Quilt (page 122) or use your favorite methods to layer and baste the runner top, batting, and backing.

2. Quilt as desired. I did simple outline quilting on the curves.

3. Bind your runner using my French double-fold binding method as described in Binding (page 126) or your own preferred method.

TIP

When sewing on the binding, make sure not to cut off the design at the seam allowance around the edge!

CARNIVAL QUILT

Finished size: 71" × 71" (180 × 180cm)
Designed and pieced by Angela Pingel
Quilted by Marion McClellan

Inspired by a delightful twist on my original Petal Pushers quilt, the Carnival quilt uses bold color, improv, and large blocks for a distinct quilt that packs a punch. With 24" × 24" (61 × 61cm) blocks, this quilt comes together surprisingly quickly. The true fun comes in making every version of it completely unique with the addition of improv piecing. Don't be afraid to try improv piecing despite the initial tougher time estimating fabric needed. You will find that this is a quilt you simply cannot mess up because the charm of improv is that you create the layout as you go. **Note:** This quilt is designed to be precut friendly with a jelly roll, charm pack, and fat quarters.

MATERIALS

2½" (6.4cm) wide Jelly Roll and matching 5" (13cm) charm pack for sashing fabric (white is used in book quilt)

8 distinct solid color fabric collections in three tones each for a total of 24–32 fat quarters (46 × 56cm). Colors used in quilt in book are Pink, Purple, Orange, Yellow, Grass Green, Kelly Green, Aqua, and Blue

- Solid light tone: one fat quarter (46 × 56cm)
- Solid medium tone: one fat quarter (46 × 56cm)
- Solid dark tone: 1–2 fat quarters (46 × 56cm)

Additional print scraps in each color with minimum width of 2½" (6.4cm) for improv pieces as desired. If only using 1 solid dark tone for the darkest ring, add a second fat quarter of the same fabric.

½ yd binding fabric (46cm)

4½ yds backing fabric (411.5cm)

80" × 80" batting (203 × 203cm)

TOOLS

Templates E and F

Template plastic or paper

See page 116 for Improv Piecing and Cutting instructions.

This quilt top is formed from eight quilt blocks, four of which are kept intact and four of which are cut in pairs along diagonals for the outer edge blocks. The four which are cut will be divided into two groups of two with one set cut vertically through the block on point and one set cut horizontally through the block on point.

CUTTING

WOF = width of fabric

FROM EACH OF THE 8 SOLID LIGHT TONE FQS:

- Cut 4 squares 4½" x 4½" (11.5 x 11.5cm).
  - Subcut 2 pieces F from 2 squares.

FROM EACH OF THE 8 SOLID MEDIUM TONE FQS:

- Cut 2 squares 4½" x 4½" (11.5 x 11.5cm).
  - Subcut into 2 pieces F.
- Cut 2 strips 4½" x 8½" (11.5 x 20cm).
- Cut 2 strips 4½" x 12½" (11.5 x 32cm) (a great place to add improv patchwork if desired).
- Cut 2 squares 5" x 5" (13 x 13cm).
  - Subcut into 2 pieces E.

FROM EACH OF THE 8 SOLID DARK TONE FQS:

- Cut 2 squares 4½" x 4½" (11.5 x 11.5cm).
  - Subcut into 2 pieces F.
- Cut 2 strips 4½" x 16½" (11.5 x 42cm).
- Cut 2 strips 4½" x 20½" (11.5 x 51cm) (a great place to add improv patchwork if desired).
- Cut 2 squares 5" x 5" (13 x 13cm).
  - Subcut into 2 pieces E.

FROM JELLY ROLL SASHING FABRIC:

- Cut 16 strips 2½" x 24½" (6.5 x 62cm.
- Cut 13 squares 2½" x 2½" (6.5 x 6.5cm).

FROM MATCHING CHARM PACK SASHING FABRIC:

- Cut 16 pieces E.

FROM BINDING FABRIC:

- Cut 7 strips 2¼" (6cm) x WOF.

FROM BACKING FABRIC:

- Cut 2 rectangles 2¼ yds (206cm) x WOF.

IMPROV PIECING

This quilt uses very simple improv piecing to add dimension and interest to a standard repeating block. The ultimate goal of improvisational piecing is to create the needed piece or strip through a combination of unmeasured and randomly placed extra fabrics. In this quilt, I use shades of solid fabrics as my starting point and add in prints in an improv fashion. Inserting prints is a great way to show off special pieces of fabric. I used tonally aligned print fabrics in my quilt, but you can also take this opportunity to add a pop of a contrasting color. You can use straight-cut lines or angled cuts to connect your fabric within your strips. It is completely up to you. That's the beauty of improv. Sometimes I use an entire strip from another fabric and other times I use a patchwork pieced strip with a combination of solids and prints. Remember you just need to get the cut lengths listed in the next section. How you get there is your choice.

IDEAS FOR IMPROV PIECING A STRIP TOGETHER

It should be noted that one solid dark tone fat quarter is not enough to cut all the pieces used in the dark outer ring. The cutting instructions include suggested places to add prints to fill out the needed measurements. If you do want a predominantly solid dark tone ring, then get a second fat quarter of that particular color. Otherwise, you will need a coordinating print fat quarter for the solid dark tone fabric.

Remember, this is supposed to be fun and freeing! Don't get too worried about fabric amounts and play with what you have. The rules are meant to be broken.

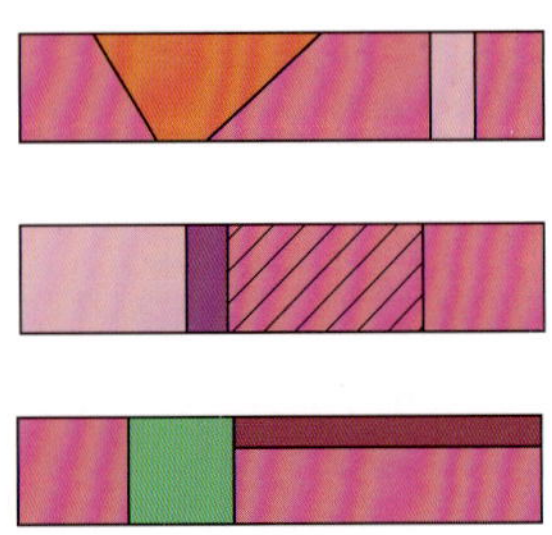

Improv strip piecing is about breaking the rules to create something unique.

PIECING THE BLOCKS

Unfinished block size: 24" × 24" (61 × 61cm)
This quilt has eight blocks in different colors. Instructions are for one block in a single color. Repeat the following steps 1–10 for all eight blocks.

INNER RING

1. Sew together solid light tone piece F with solid medium tone piece E. Press seams toward F. Trim block to 4½" × 4½" (11.5 × 11.5cm) with ¼" (0.6cm) seam allowance on piece E. Repeat for two sets of EF light/medium tone modern ¼-circle curve blocks **(fig. 1)**.

2. To assemble the Inner Ring, gather both solid light tone fabric 4½" × 4½" (11.5 × 11.5cm) squares and the two EF sets made in Step 1. Sew the 4½" × 4½" (11.5 × 11.5cm) squares to the EF sets orientated as shown **(fig. 2)**. Press the seams towards solid squares. Sew the two pairs together, aligning center seams **(fig. 2)**. Press the seam open.

MIDDLE RING

3. With the Inner Ring block oriented as shown **(fig. 3)**, sew a solid medium tone rectangle 4½" × 8½" (11.5 × 20cm) to the left and right sides. Press the seams toward the rectangles.

4. Sew together solid medium tone piece F with solid dark tone piece E. Press seams toward F. Trim block to 4½" × 4½" (11.5 × 11.5cm) with ¼" (0.6cm) seam allowance on piece E. Repeat for two sets of EF medium/dark tone modern ¼-circle curve blocks as in Step 1 **(fig. 1)**.

5. Sew the EF sets made in Step 4 to the solid medium tone rectangle 4½" × 12½" (11.5 × 32cm) orientated as shown **(fig. 4)**. Press the seams toward the long rectangles.

6. Sew the strips from Step 5 to the top and bottom of the sets created in Step 3, orientated as shown **(fig. 5)**. Press the seams toward the solid medium tone rectangles.

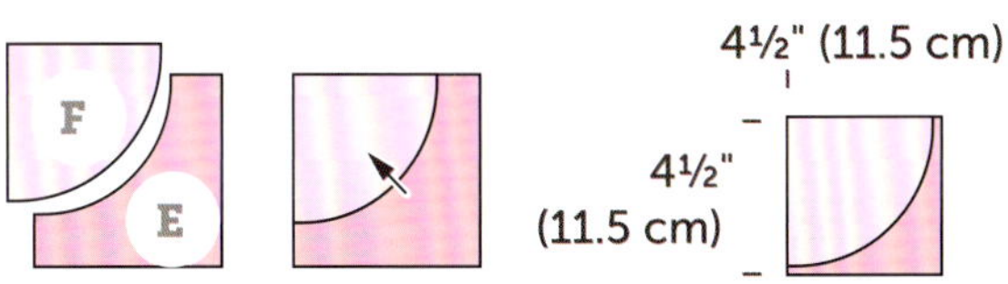

figure 1

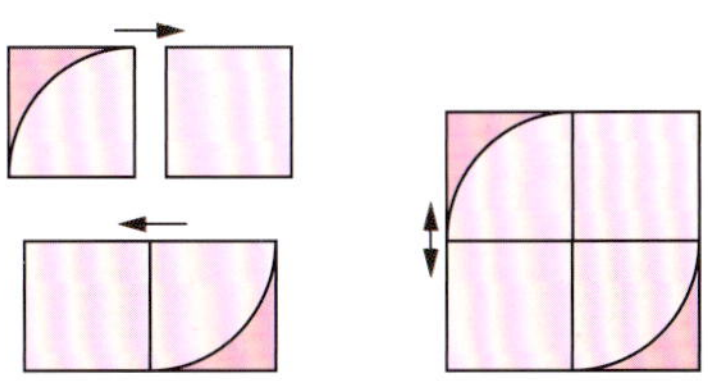
figure 2

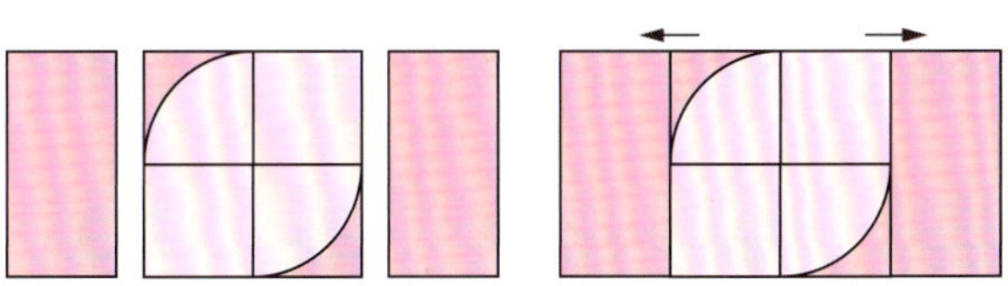
figure 3

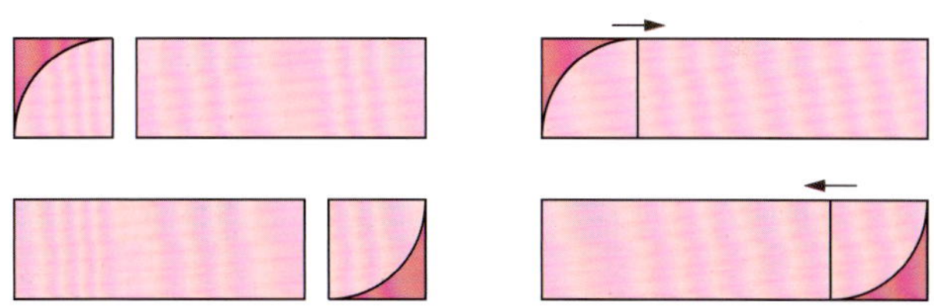
figure 4

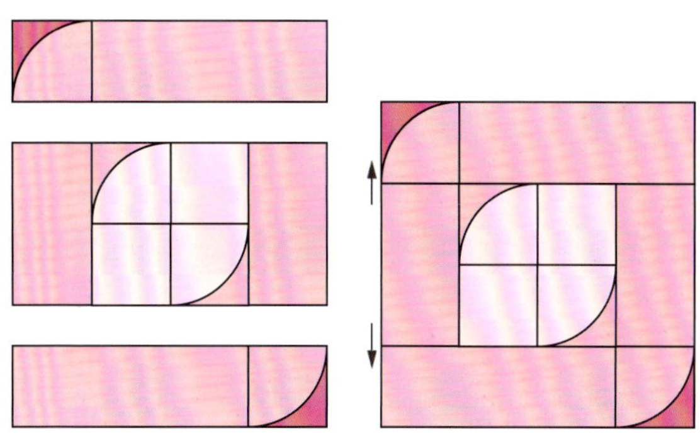
figure 5

OUTER RING

7. Sew together solid dark tone piece F with sashing piece E. Press seams toward F. Trim block to 4½" × 4½" (11.5 × 11.5cm) with ¼" (0.6cm) seam allowance on piece E. Repeat for two sets of EF dark tone/white modern ¼-circle curve blocks as in Step 1 **(fig. 1)**.

8. With the Middle Ring block orientated as shown **(fig. 6)**, sew a solid dark tone rectangle 4½" × 16½" (11.5 x42cm) to the left and right sides. Press the seams toward the rectangles.

9. Sew the EF sets made in Step 7 to the solid dark tone rectangle 4½" × 20½" (11.5 × 51cm) orientated as shown **(fig. 7)**. Press the seams toward the long rectangles.

10. Sew the strips from Step 9 to the top and bottom of the sets created in Step 8, orientated as shown **(fig. 8)**. Press the seams toward the solid dark tone rectangles.

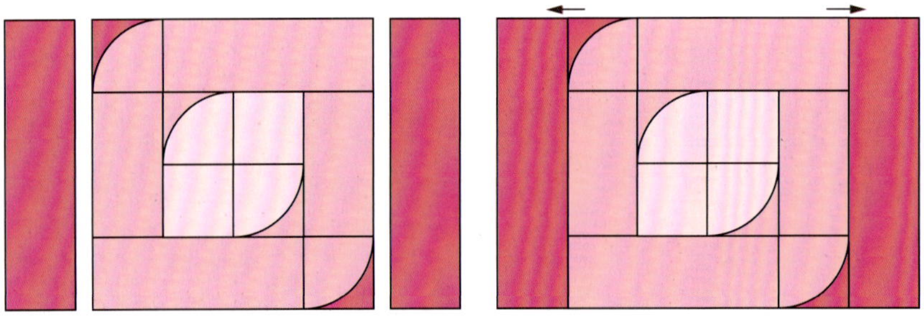

figure 6

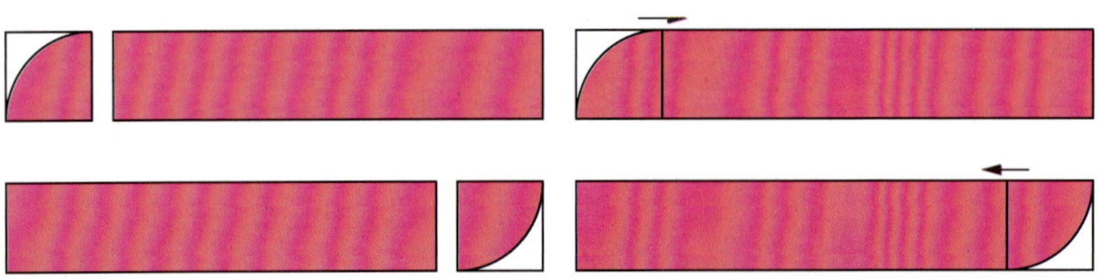

figure 7

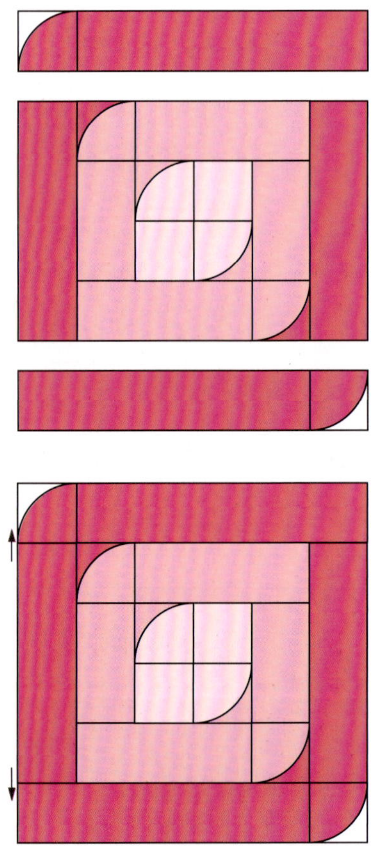

figure 8

TIP

I took individual photos of each of my blocks with my phone so I could play with their arrangement. You can do this digitally or actually print out the photos. This let me see exactly how I wanted to orient each block and where to cut the edge blocks. I found it extremely helpful. Another helpful method is to alternate warm and cool color blocks. That will help keep the quilt balanced. I saved some of my most vibrant color blocks for the edges as they would be cut in half and therefore give two smaller pops of color rather than one large block. I used my comfort colors for the blocks in the center as I knew I would love these in their entirety.

MAKING THE QUILT TOP

1. Refer to the Carnival Construction Diagram for assembly of the quilt blocks and sashing with corner stones into a quilt top.

2. Lay out your blocks together on point to determine which four you will be keeping intact for the center of the quilt and which four you will be cutting for the edges of the quilt.

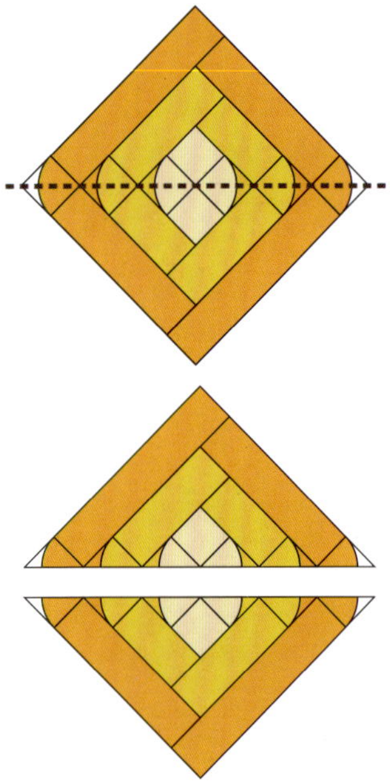

figure 10

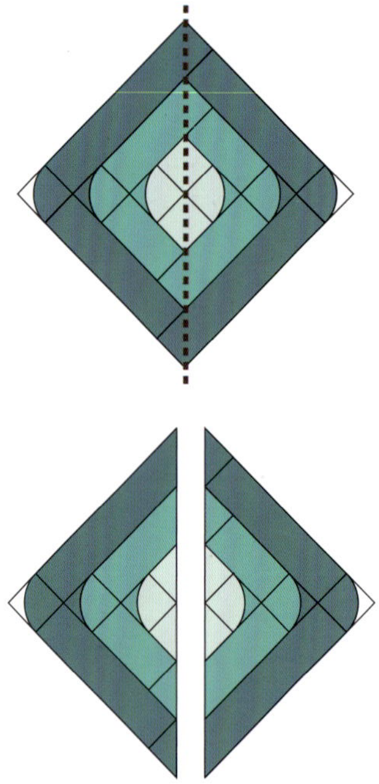

figure 11

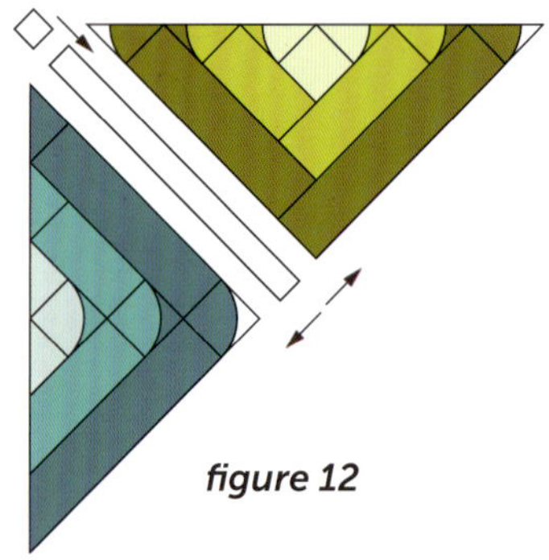

figure 12

3. Arrange the blocks in the orientation shown with the curved edges running left to right and the sharp corners meeting vertically at points. Cut the two blocks for the top and bottom of the quilt along the center horizontal line **(fig. 10)**. Cut the two blocks for the left and right edges of the quilt along the center vertical line **(fig. 11)**.

4. Create three long diagonal sashing rows with sashing strips and cornerstones together as shown along the 2½" (6.5cm) edges, alternating 2½" × 2½" (6.5 × 6.5cm) cornerstones with 2½" × 24½" (6.5 × 62cm) sashing strips. Create two rows with three cornerstones and two sashing strips. Create one row with five cornerstones and four sashing strips. Press seams toward sashing strips **(Carnival Construction Diagram)**.

5. Sew 2½" × 24½" (6.5 × 62cm) sashing strip and 2½" × 2½" (6.5 × 6.5cm) cornerstone together. Repeat for a total of two small sashing sets. Press seams toward sashing strips.

6. Sew sashing sets created in Step 5 between the upper left two corner blocks and lower right two corner blocks with the cornerstone on the outside as shown. Press seams toward sashing **(fig. 12)**. This creates rows 1 and 4.

7. Sew 2½" × 24½" (6.5 × 62cm) sashing between remaining blocks on point as shown. Press seams toward the sashing **(Carnival Construction Diagram)**.This creates rows 2 and 3.

8. Sew the three long diagonal sashing rows created in Step 4 in between rows 1 and 2, rows 2 and 3, and rows 3 and 4, aligning seams and cornerstones **(Carnival Construction Diagram)**.

9. Square up the quilt top and trim excess cornerstone fabric from the edges.

FINISHING

1. Refer to Finishing your Quilt (page 122) or use your favorite methods to layer and baste the quilt top, batting, and backing.

2. Quilt as desired. Longarm quilter Marion McClellan custom quilted my quilt with a mix of freehand geometric designs to accentuate the movement in each block.

3. Bind your quilt using my French double-fold binding method as described in Binding (page 126) or your own method as preferred.

CARNIVAL CONSTRUCTION DIAGRAM

FINISHING YOUR QUILT

After you have completed your quilt top, there is still the matter of turning it into an actual quilt. To finish up your beautiful project, you will need to prepare a backing, choose the perfect batting, and layer them together. Then choose your favorite quilting design to quilt together your layers. Finally, bind the edges. You probably have your own preferred methods and techniques for all these steps in the process. If you're new to quilting, you can consult the many excellent books and websites that describe these basics. In this section, I share with you my own particular preferences and techniques.

BACKINGS

Quilt backings are such a personal thing. I know some people who put so much work into their quilt backs that the quilt is essentially two-sided. Others are just grateful to be finished with the quilt top, and they whip together something as quickly as possible. For the ultimate quick backing, you can use a single length of extra-wide backing fabric (106"–108" [269–274cm]) but admittedly the choices for these are limited. An alternative—almost as quick—is a backing pieced from standard 42" (106.5cm) width fabric, pieced with a single seam. This is the option I have used in the yardage requirements for the projects in this book—one long piece of fabric cut in half and seamed together lengthwise.

There are so many beautiful options when it comes to backing fabrics. Select one or create a patchwork of many.

PIECED OPTIONS

There are a number of pieced backing options that are slightly more complex than a single fabric. I'll admit that I often fall back on these options because I don't have the yardage needed for a large quilt back, which often requires between 5 and 6 yards (4.6–5.5m) of fabric. Using pieced multiple fabrics gives me a chance to use some of the cuts I've stashed away—those that don't seem to have a home with other fabrics, perhaps because of their color or the scale of the print, and those that make me question why I purchased them in the first place. I can also use those fabrics I just can't bear to chop up.

So, consider these options for your project. Although I don't give you measurements here because they will vary with the project, the following are a few ideas. You are only limited by your imagination! Backings can be as simple as you like or as creatively complex as you like. It's entirely up to you and your personal preferences.

OPTION 1
Four large cuts pieced to meet at the quilt back center.

OPTION 2
A strip pieced horizontally into a single seamed pieced back. This is a useful option when you have a good amount of yardage but not quite enough. It gives you the extra length you need.

OPTION 3
A back composed of fat quarters. I often end up with a collection of fat quarters that I'm not quite sure what to do with. The bonus with these is that they can be from the same fabric line and have a natural cohesion.

OPTION 4
A back that uses up those extra blocks you may have made for the quilt front. Waste not, want not! Put those blocks to good use and enjoy them, even on the back.

BATTING

Today, there are choices galore for quilt batting. With a number of manufacturers, the options get better and better all the time. Gone are the days when all quilts were made with polyester high-loft battings (although I personally still have a soft spot for this type of batting). You can choose from cotton, bamboo, soy, polyester, wool, and many combinations of these. There are "green" options for the environmentally minded. Use the batting you prefer. The quilts in this book are made from all different substrates of batting. My personal preference these days leans strongly toward wool. I love the texture it gives and the warmth it provides. (Admittedly, as I write this I'm particularly cold, so it could be coloring my view!)

BASTING

Quilts have traditionally been hand basted or secured with curved safety pins laboriously placed every few inches across the entire quilt. These pins then need to be removed as you quilt the layers. I started with this method and used it successfully to make many quilts. But frankly, I found this to be difficult on my knees and painfully slow. Eventually I made my way to the world of spray basting. And I'll never go back.

Spray basting has made quilting so much easier for me. I've tried a number of brands, and all I can say is that you get what you pay for. If you've tried this method without success, give it a try again with another brand. Follow the instructions for proper ventilation, and prepare yourself to be amazed at how quickly you can "baste" a quilt.

These days, there are so many different kinds of batting to choose from, like wool, bamboo, or cotton.

QUILTING

For the quilts in this book, I used a combination of quilting techniques. I quilted many of the projects on my domestic sewing machine. Others were quilted by the very talented professional Krista Withers on her longarm machine.

Deciding whether to do the quilting yourself on a domestic machine or to send it to a professional for quilting on a longarm machine is a very personal choice. I love the treat of sending off a large quilt top to a longarm quilter and letting her work her magic on it. It can be expensive, especially for custom work, but it's never a decision that I have regretted. Large quilts, in particular, are much easier to quilt on a longarm machine than on a domestic machine. With longarm quilting, it becomes feasible for most of us to finish the king-sized quilts we all want to make for our own beds. If you go the longarm route, you can choose a custom quilt design and let the talent of your chosen quilter shine. Or you can choose one of the available longarm pantograph designs, which are typically allover patterns. Make your decision based on what is the right design for your quilt and the style that is most pleasing to you.

Most of us, however—unless we have unlimited funds and/or access to a longarm machine—will be quilting our own quilts on a domestic machine. Although it is outside the scope of this book to offer detailed information about quilting, I'll review the basic choices.

Two methods—straight-line quilting and free-motion quilting—are the most commonly used. Simple straight-line quilting, done with a walking foot, is a tried-and-true method that really seems to work with any design, even those with curves. If you are comfortable with straight-line quilting, you can easily do a number of variations, including a crosshatch pattern and a grid.

With free-motion, you can get fancier. The idea of this technique, in which you drop your machine's feed dogs and move the quilt freely under a darning foot, is often frightening to those who haven't tried it. Yet many quilters wind up converting to it almost exclusively, because ultimately it can be a very quick method for finishing up your quilt. The options for free-motion quilting designs are too numerous to list, but basics are a simple meander stitch, spiral stitching, and loops.

There is one additional option for quilting if you have a machine with decorative stitches: use an expanded version of a simple decorative stitch. You can create waves or curves with even a simple zigzag stitch if you "max out" on stitch length and width. Play with the stitch options on your machine to see what is available, and think outside the box!

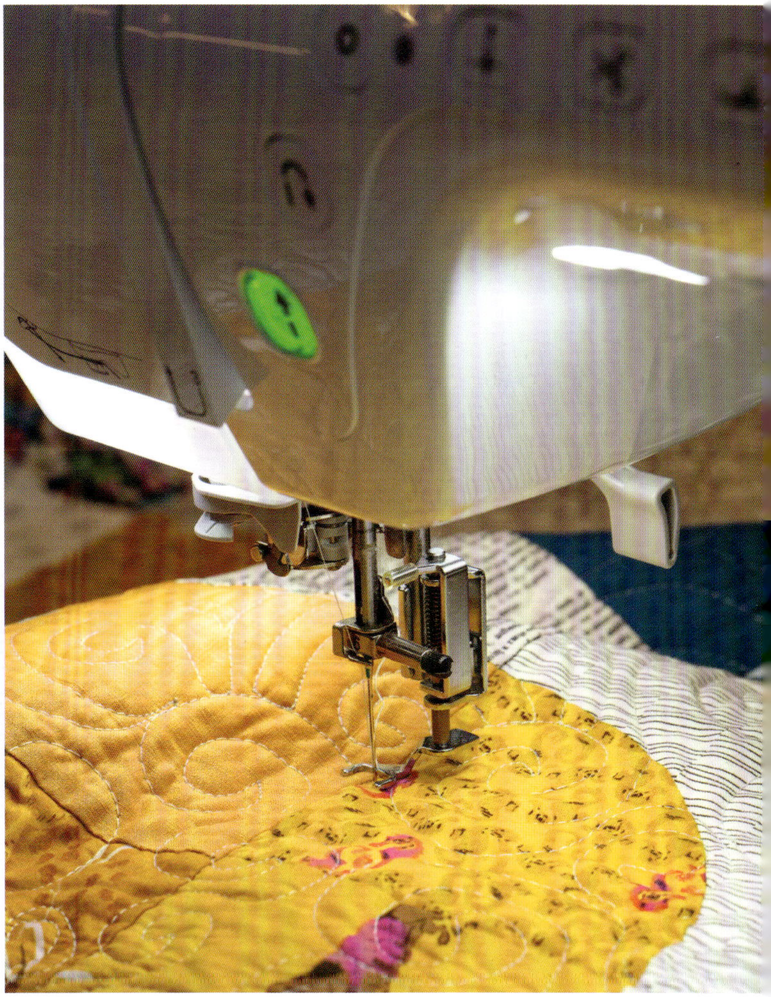

Deciding whether to do the quilting yourself or send it to a longarm quilter is a personal choice.

You can make a scrappy binding by creating strips with multiple fabrics.

BINDING

Binding is the final step in completing your quilt. It is personally one of my favorite moments with my quilt. (Let the stoning begin!) I use a French double-fold binding method that is machine sewn to the front and handsewn to the back. I love the perfect finish I get with this, and I enjoy the time spent with the quilt at the very end. I work my way around the quilt one stitch at a time, touching each edge of the quilt for one last time.

To make the binding, first cut the necessary number of strips 2½" (6.5cm) × WOF. You will find this number in the cutting list for each project in this book. You can cut all these strips from one fabric, or create a scrappy binding by using multiple fabrics. (This is a great way to add to your fabric if you don't have quite enough for the binding.) If you so choose, you may cut these strips on the bias for a bias binding. I usually don't bother with a bias binding unless I will be binding a curved edge.

MAKING A FRENCH DOUBLE-FOLD BINDING

1. Sew the strips together using diagonal seams to create one long strip of fabric **(fig. 1)**. Place the ends of two strips perpendicular, right sides together. Sew a diagonal seam from the upper left corner to the bottom right corner. Trim away the excess fabric to leave a ¼" (6mm) seam allowance. Press the seam open.

2. Fold the binding strip wrong sides together along the length, and press.

3. To sew the binding to the quilt, place the binding strip on the quilt top, aligning the binding strip raw edges with the quilt edge. Do not start in a corner, but rather in the middle of one side. Leave a 5" (12.5cm) tail unsewn at the beginning of the binding **(fig. 2)**. Stitch the binding to the quilt using a generous ¼" (6mm) seam allowance.

4. When you near a corner of the quilt, stop stitching ¼" (6mm) from the end. Optional: Turn the quilt and stitch the binding from the stopping point to the corner at a 45-degree angle **(fig. 3)**.

5. Remove the quilt from the machine, and fold back the binding, aligning the raw edges of the binding with the raw edge of the quilt **(fig. 4)**.

6. Fold the binding back down, matching the folded edge of the binding with the quilt top **(fig. 5)**. Continue sewing along the edge of the quilt. Repeat Steps 4– 6 for all corners.

7. As you near the end of the binding and approach the tail you left at the beginning, stop stitching about 10" (25.5cm) from the initial stitches.

8. Trim the binding so that the edges of the first tail overlap the end tail by 2½" (6.5cm) **(fig. 6)**.

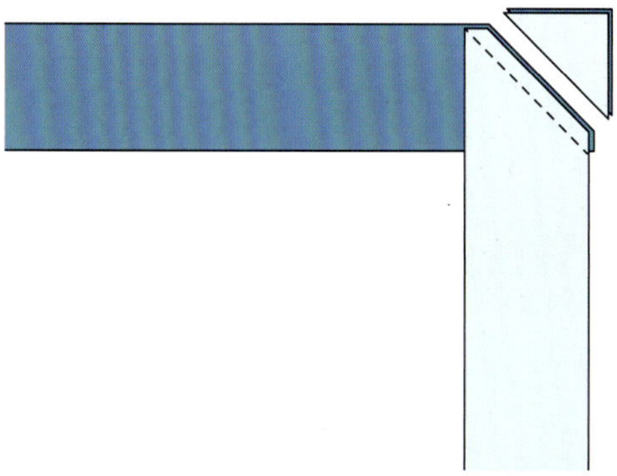

figure 1

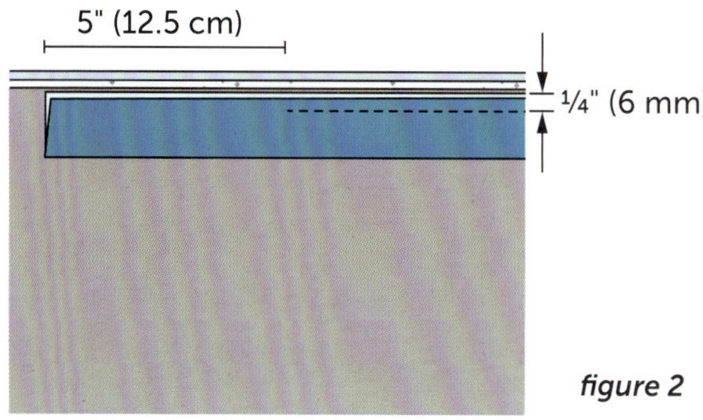

figure 2

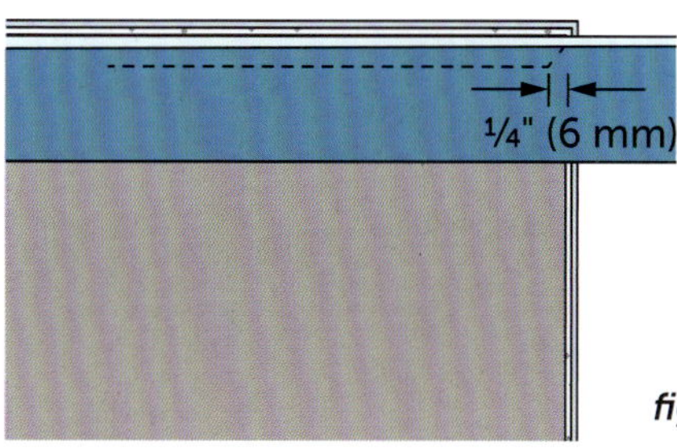

figure 3

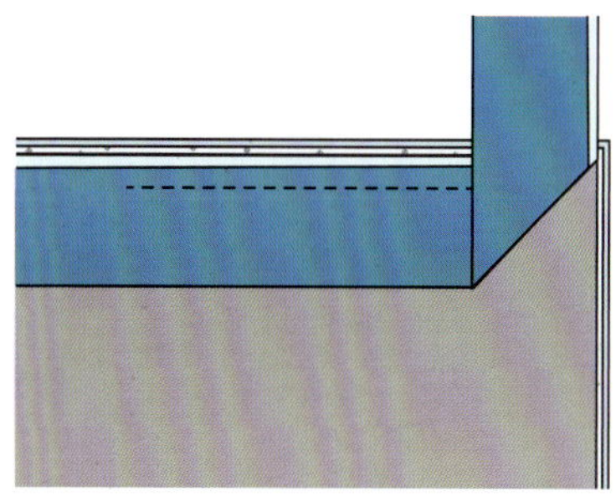

figure 4

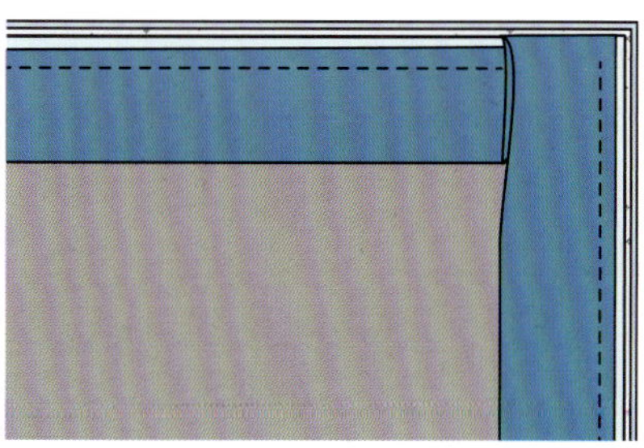

figure 5

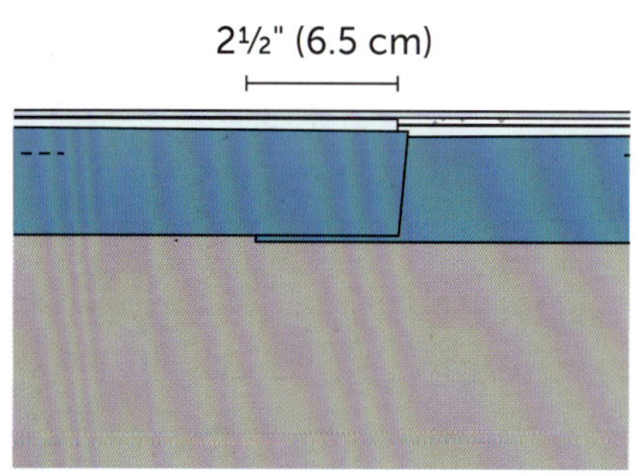

figure 6

9. Open the binding tails and lay the fabrics right sides together, placing the beginning tail end over the ending tail end, just as you did to piece the strips together. Pin. You will most likely need to squish the quilt together under the binding as you work. Don't be afraid to do this. Sew a diagonal seam from the upper left-hand corner to the bottom right-hand corner as shown **(fig. 7)**.

10. Trim the excess fabric leaving a ¼" (6mm) seam allowance. Press the seam open. Fold the binding back in half, wrong sides together, and stitch it in place along the edge of the quilt.

11. Flip the folded edge of the binding to the back of the quilt and hold it in place with spring clips such as Clover Wonder Clips. With a needle and thread, hand sew the binding in place, using a small, hidden stitch.

12. To miter the corners of the binding, first fold the binding along the stitched edge and hand crease an angle into the binding **(fig. 8)**.

13. Fold the angled, folded edge of the binding back over the corner, and handstitch it in place **(fig. 9)**. Continue stitching around the entire quilt perimeter.

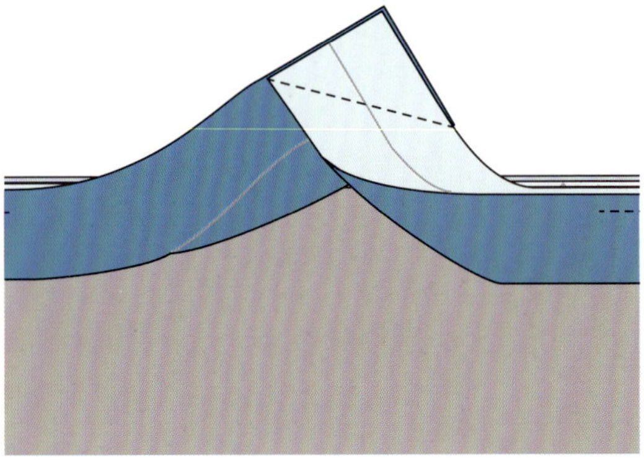

figure 7

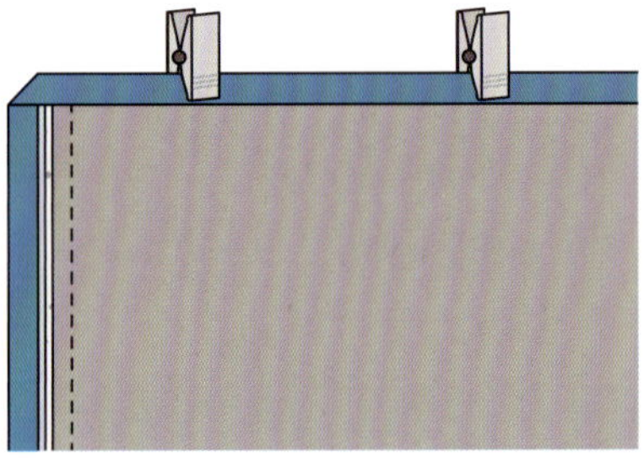

figure 8

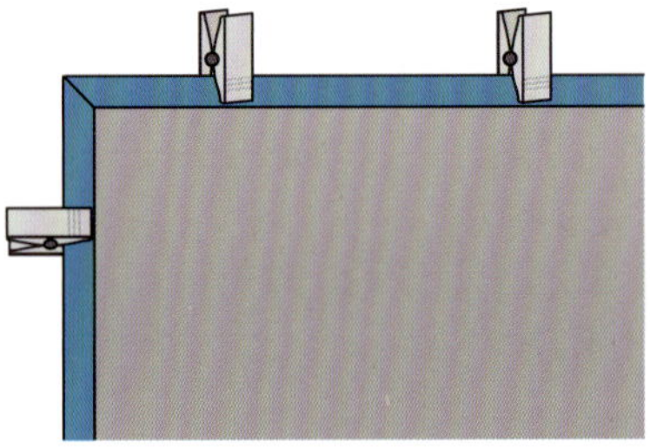

figure 9

TEMPLATES

Some template patterns are oversized compared to the finished dimensions to allow for trimming the finished block to size. Note the gray trim lines on some patterns for the modern block pieces.

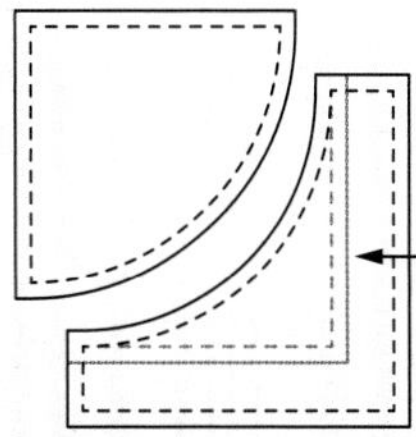

Modern block

PROJECT NAME	PAGE NUMBER	TEMPLATES
SIP AND STITCH COASTERS	22	B
PAIR OF PILLOWS	28	A, B
MEDALLION BABY QUILT	36	C, D
TENNIS MATCH QUILT	40	A, B, E, F
ARABIAN NIGHTS QUILT	46	G, H
PAINT DRIP QUILT	52	G, H, J, K
NINE PATCH CURVES QUILT	60	I, F
CAT EYE QUILT	68	N, O
FLOWER POWER QUILT	74	A, B, C, D
FULL BLOOM QUILT	80	C, D
BUTTERFLIES QUILT	86	G, H, P, Q, N, O
BRIGHT IDEAS WALL HANGING	94	G, H, R, S, T, U, V, W
ORNAMENTAL QUILT	102	E, F, L, M
SUNRISE TABLE RUNNER	108	E, F
CARNIVAL QUILT	114	E, F

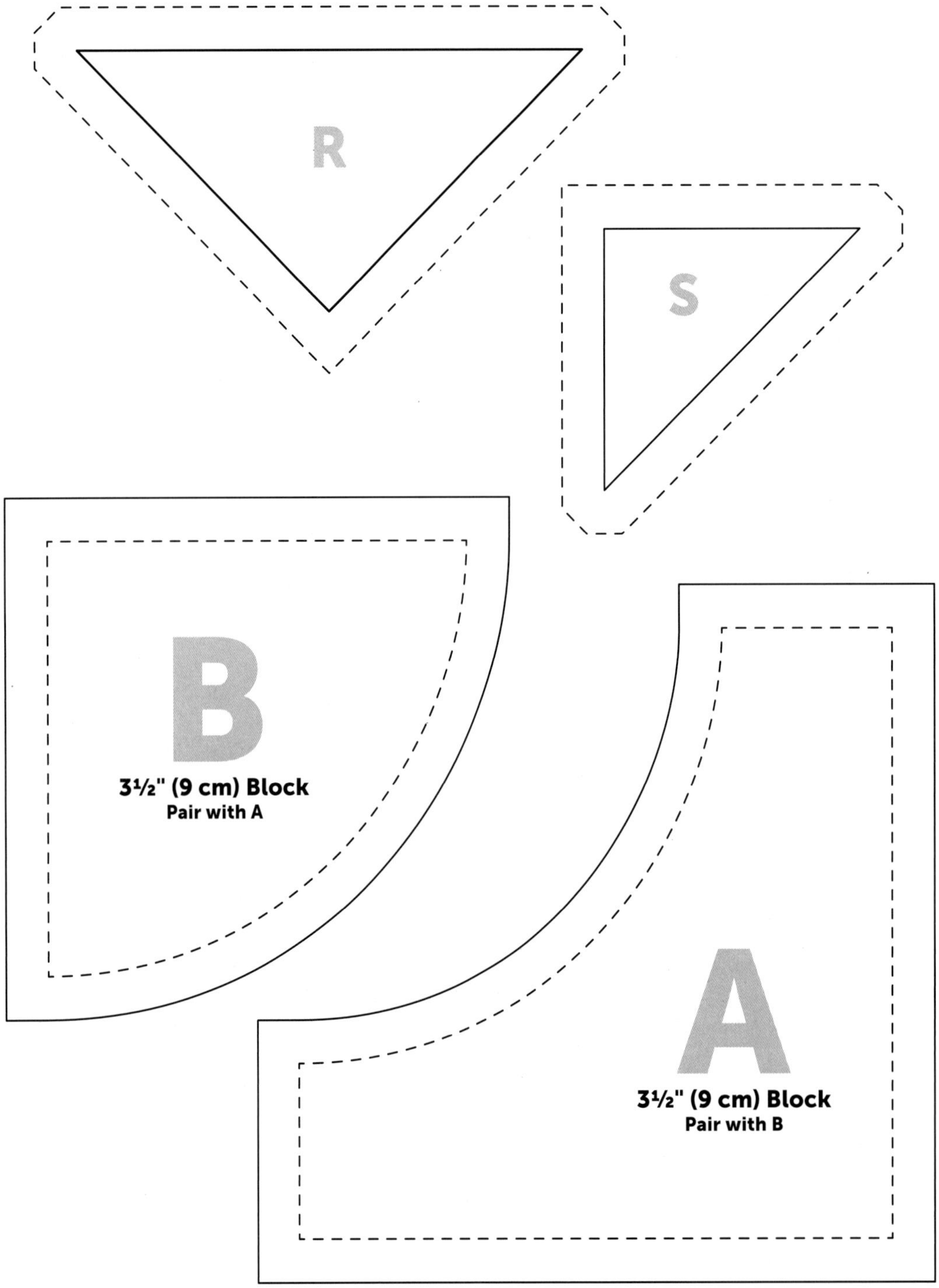
R
S
B
3½" (9 cm) Block
Pair with A
A
3½" (9 cm) Block
Pair with B

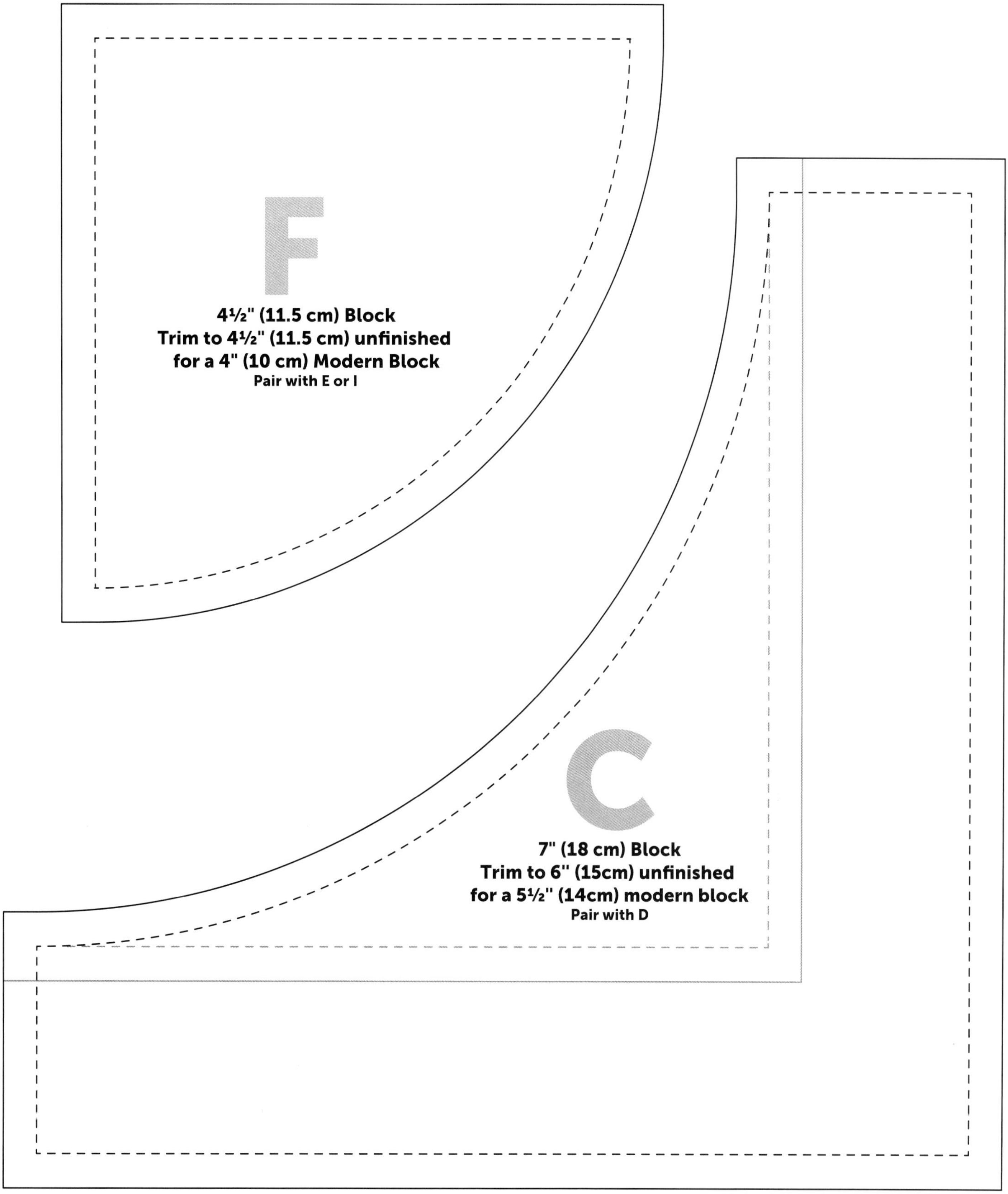
F
4½" (11.5 cm) Block
Trim to 4½" (11.5 cm) unfinished
for a 4" (10 cm) Modern Block
Pair with E or I
C
7" (18 cm) Block
Trim to 6" (15cm) unfinished
for a 5½" (14cm) modern block
Pair with D

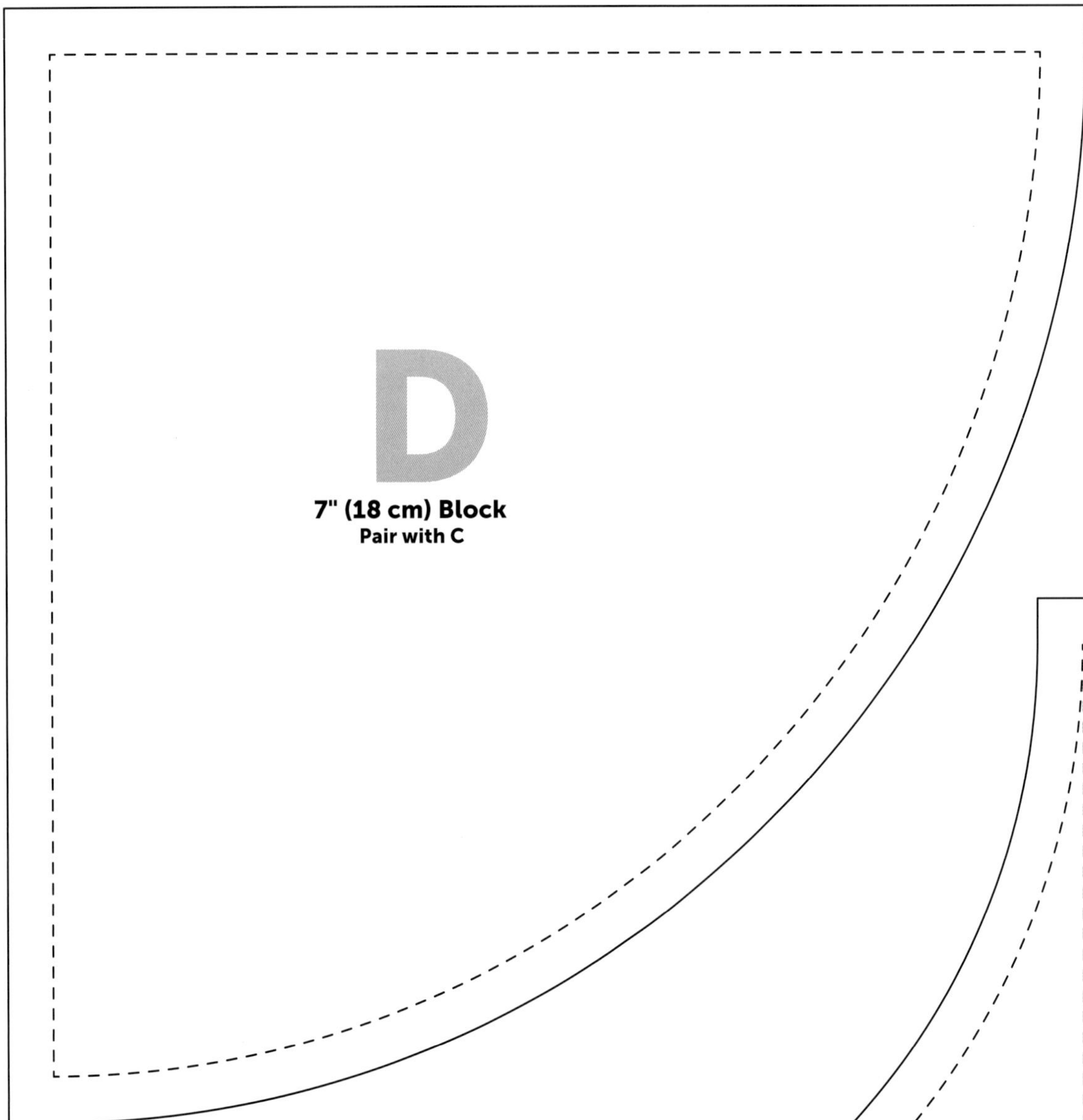
D
7" (18 cm) Block
Pair with C

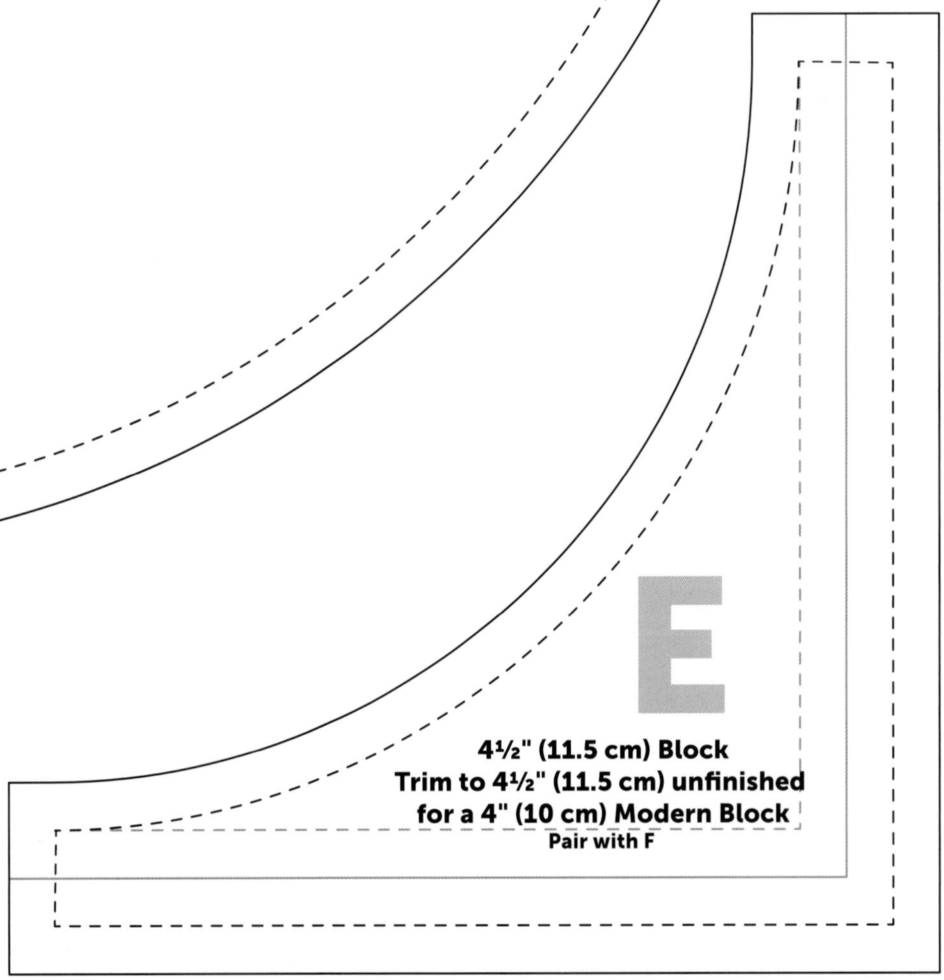
E
4½" (11.5 cm) Block
Trim to 4½" (11.5 cm) unfinished
for a 4" (10 cm) Modern Block
Pair with F

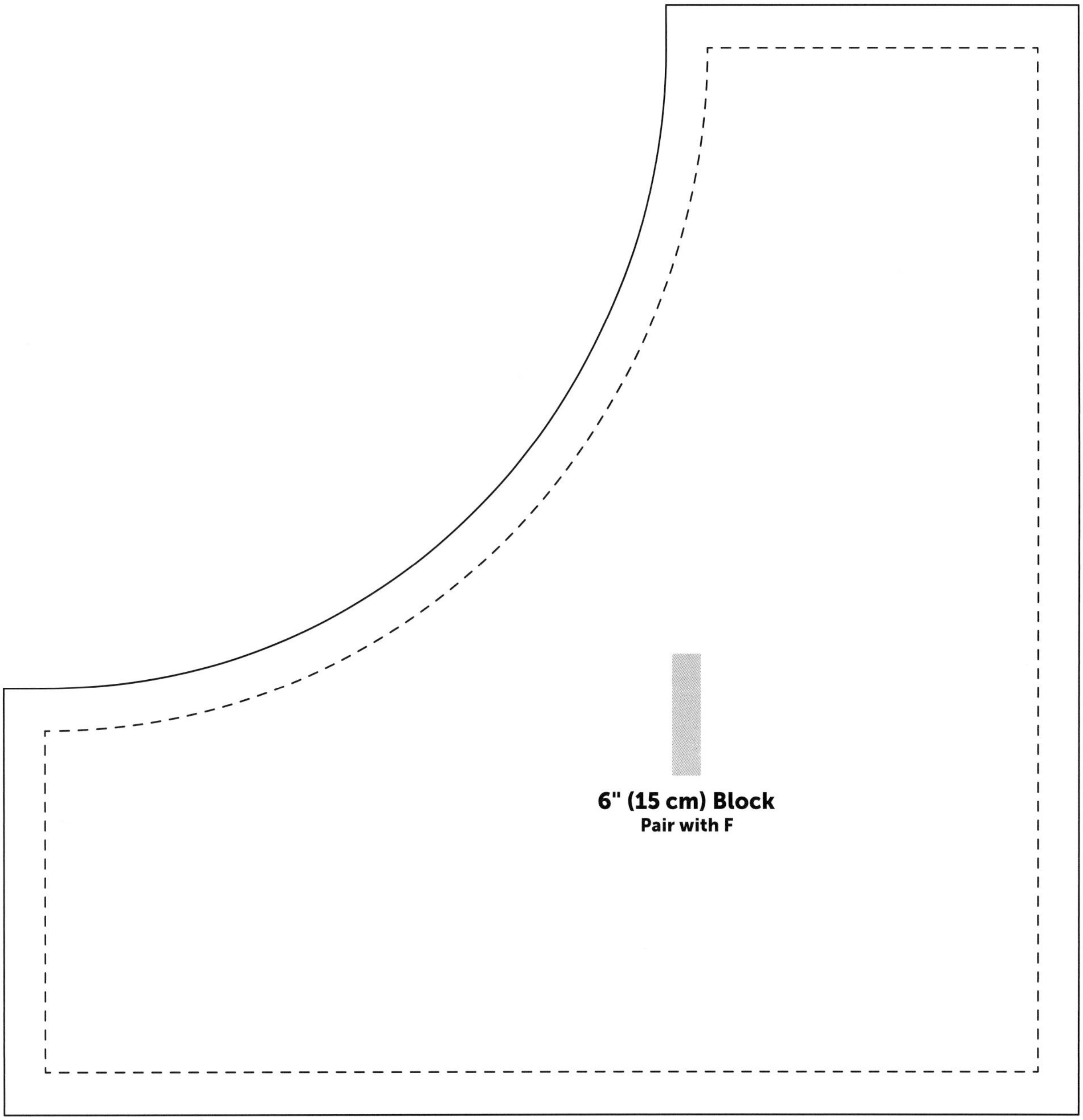
6" (15 cm) Block
Pair with F

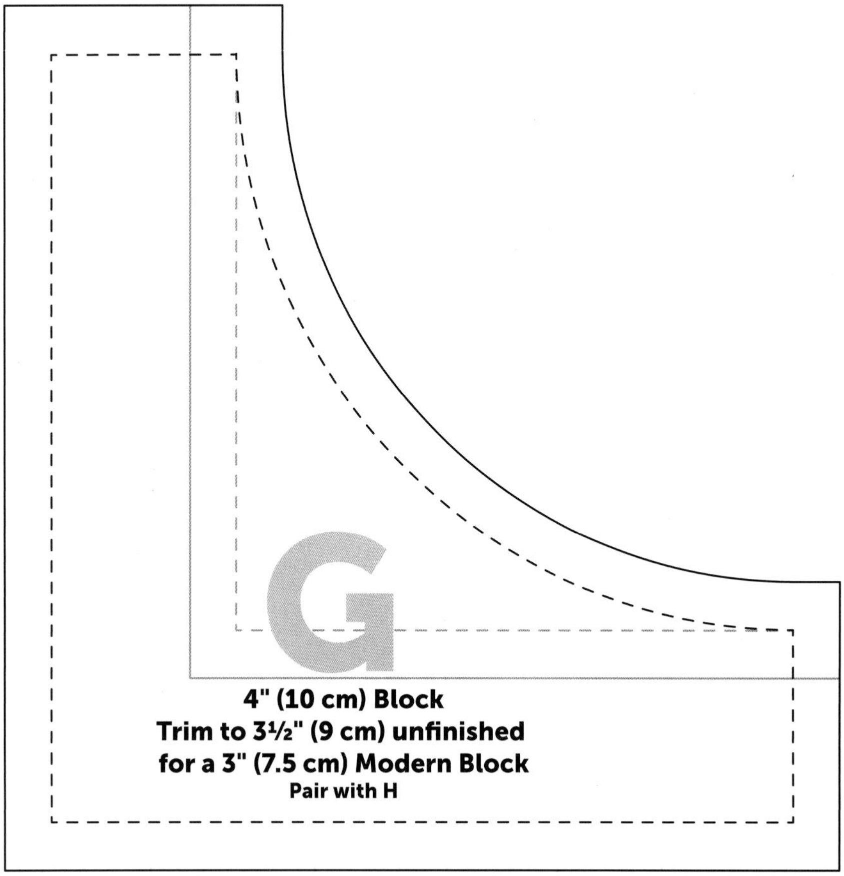
G
4" (10 cm) Block
Trim to 3½" (9 cm) unfinished
for a 3" (7.5 cm) Modern Block
Pair with H

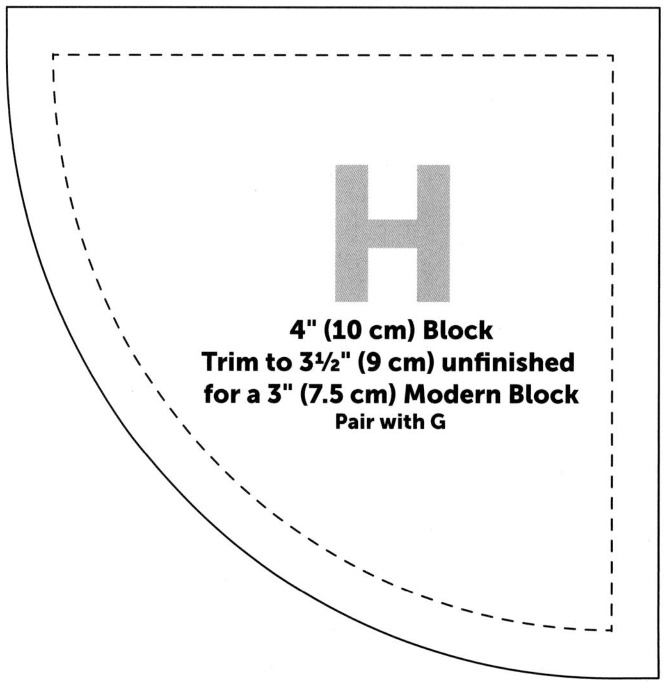
H
4" (10 cm) Block
Trim to 3½" (9 cm) unfinished
for a 3" (7.5 cm) Modern Block
Pair with G

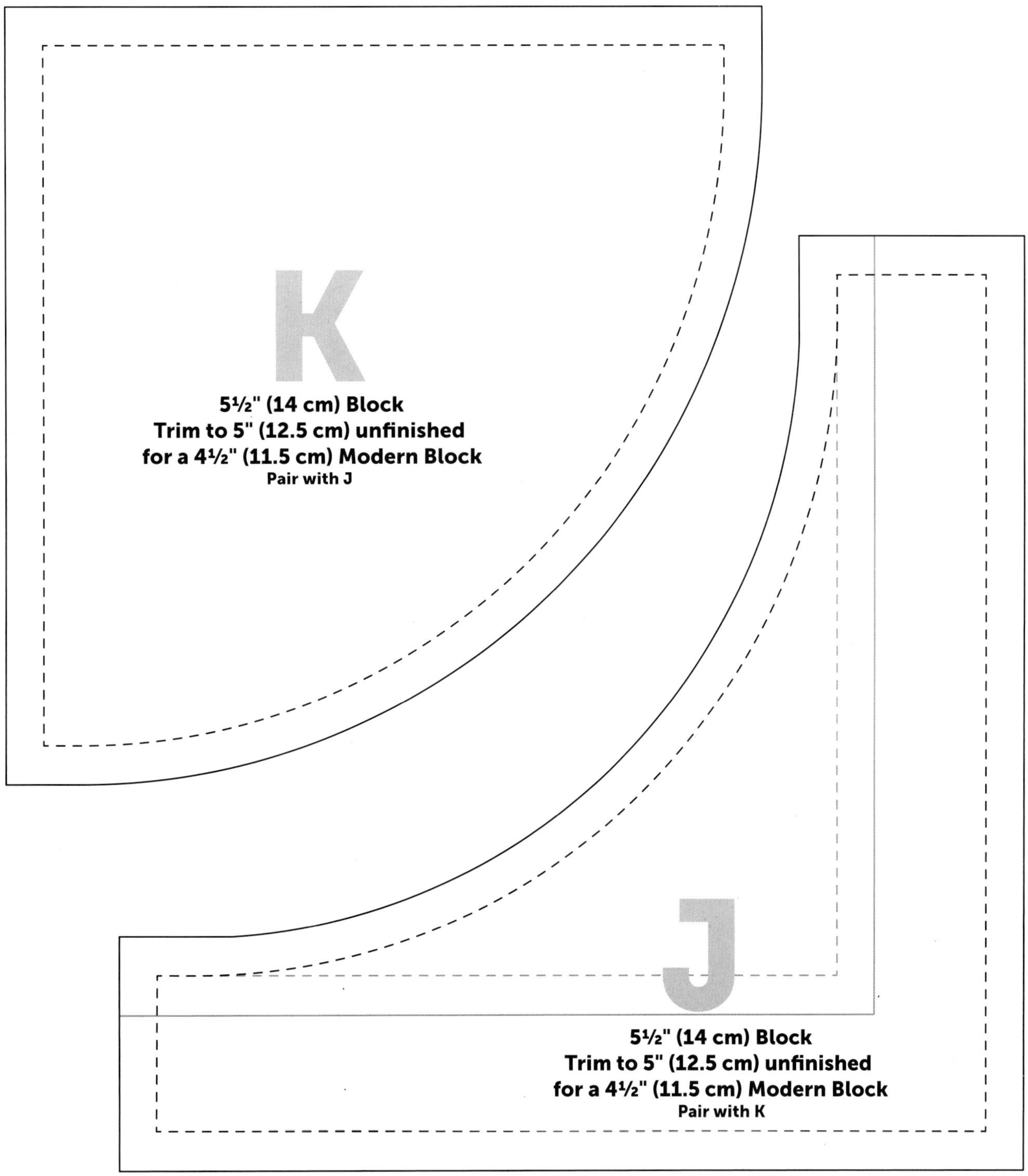
K
5½" (14 cm) Block
Trim to 5" (12.5 cm) unfinished
for a 4½" (11.5 cm) Modern Block
Pair with J
J
5½" (14 cm) Block
Trim to 5" (12.5 cm) unfinished
for a 4½" (11.5 cm) Modern Block
Pair with K

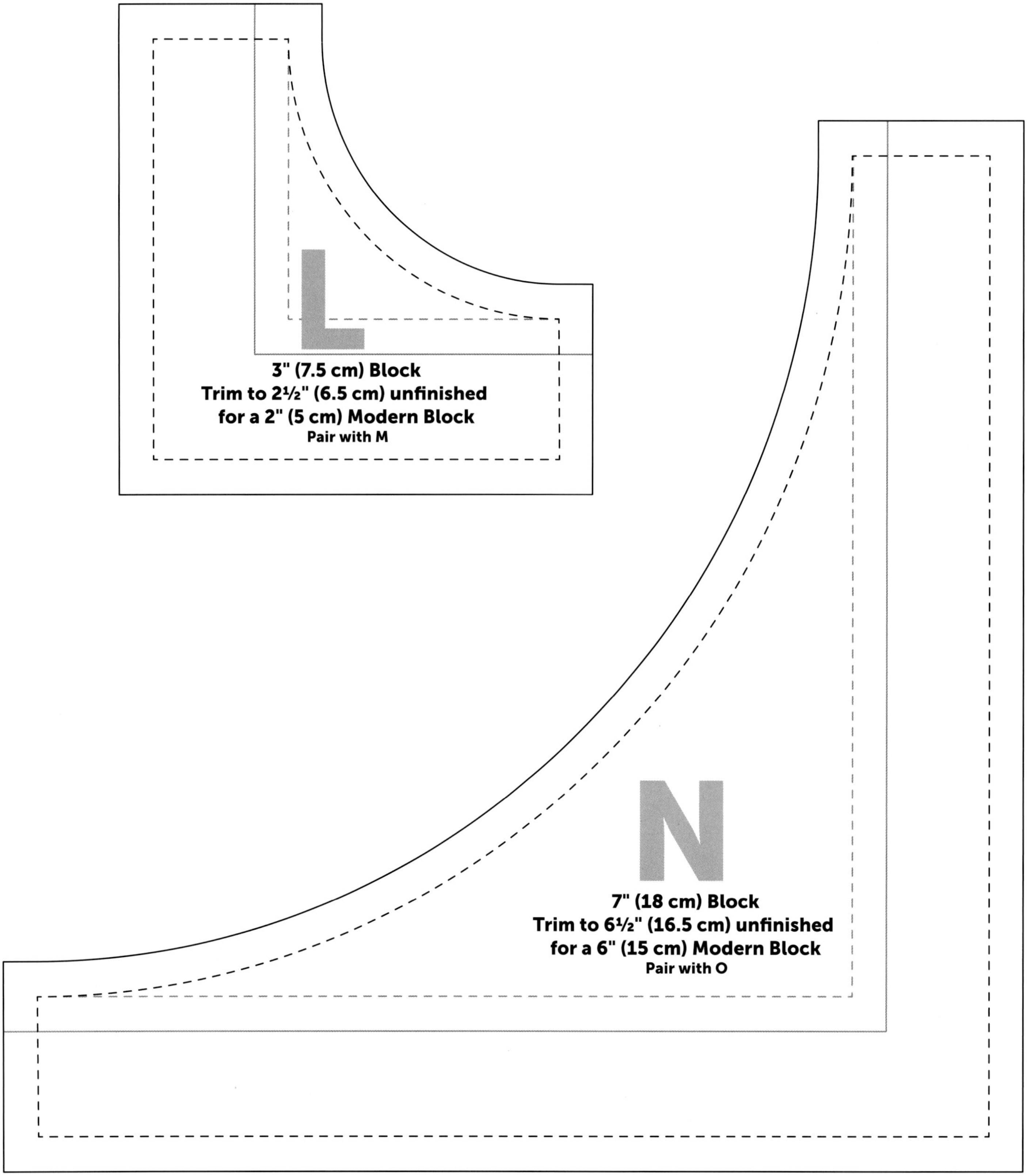
L
3" (7.5 cm) Block
Trim to 2½" (6.5 cm) unfinished
for a 2" (5 cm) Modern Block
Pair with M
N
7" (18 cm) Block
Trim to 6½" (16.5 cm) unfinished
for a 6" (15 cm) Modern Block
Pair with O

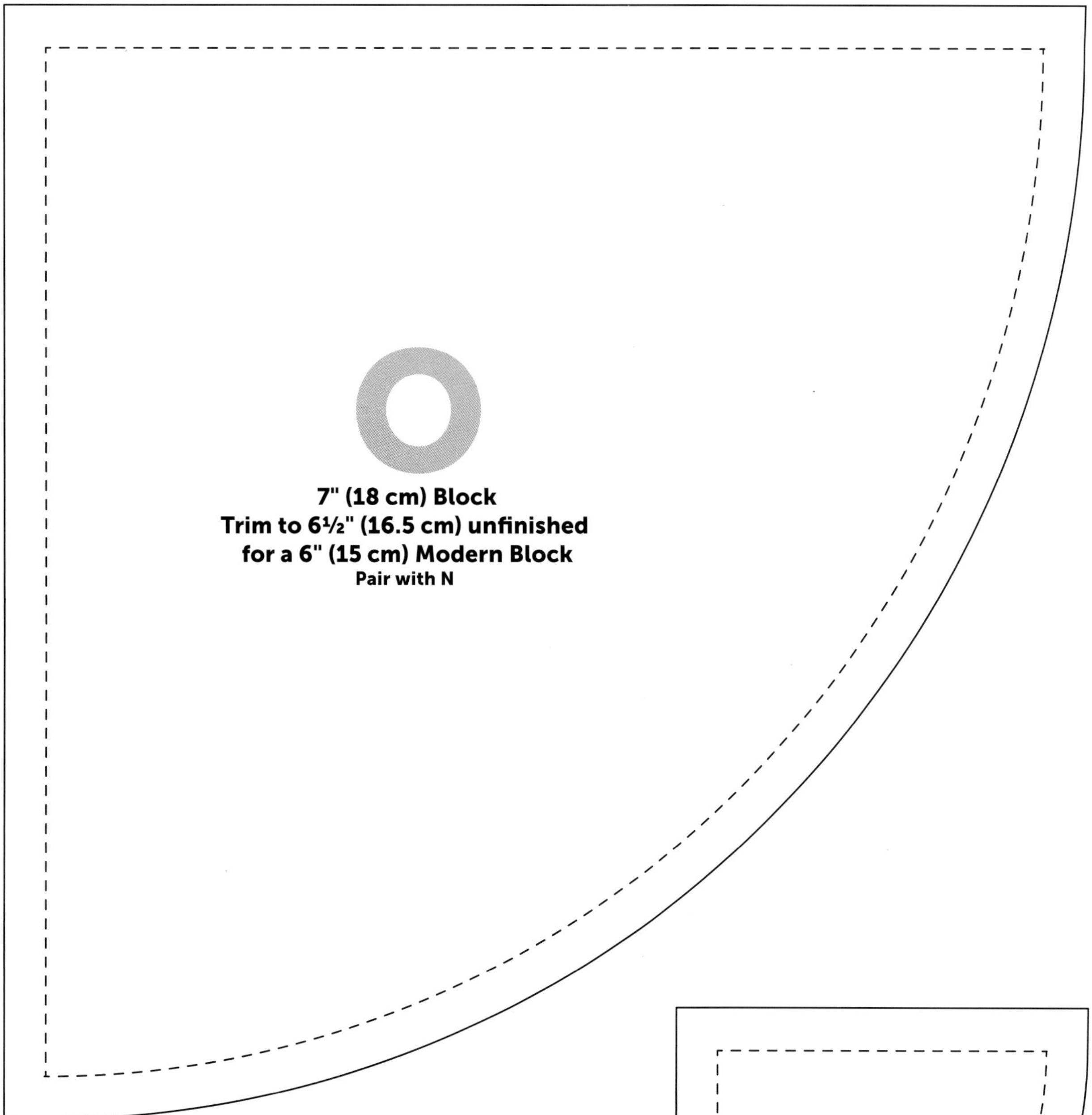

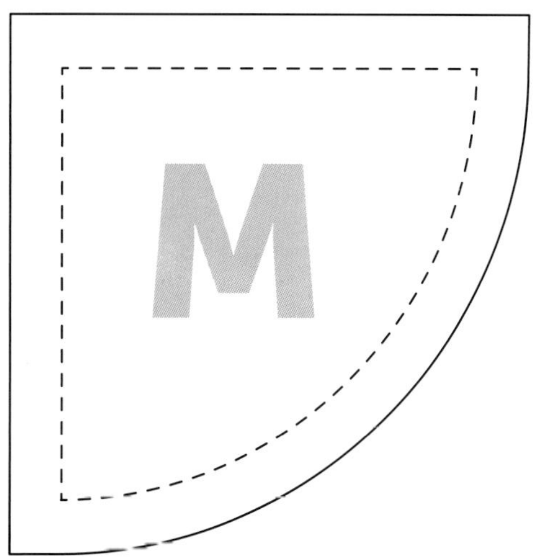

3" (7.5 cm) Block
Trim to 2½" (6.5 cm)
unfinished for a 2" (5 cm)
Modern Block
Pair with L

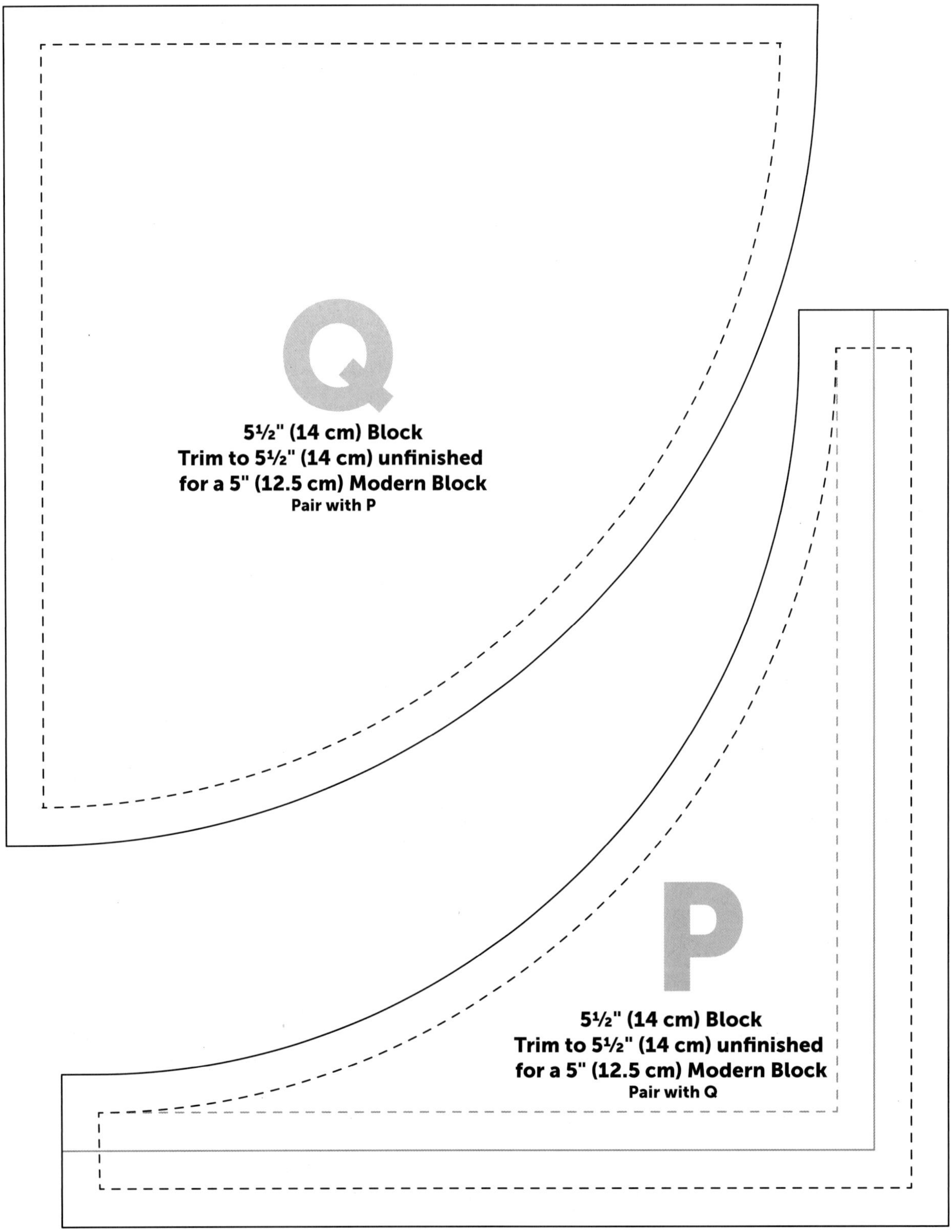
Q
5½" (14 cm) Block
Trim to 5½" (14 cm) unfinished
for a 5" (12.5 cm) Modern Block
Pair with P
P
5½" (14 cm) Block
Trim to 5½" (14 cm) unfinished
for a 5" (12.5 cm) Modern Block
Pair with Q

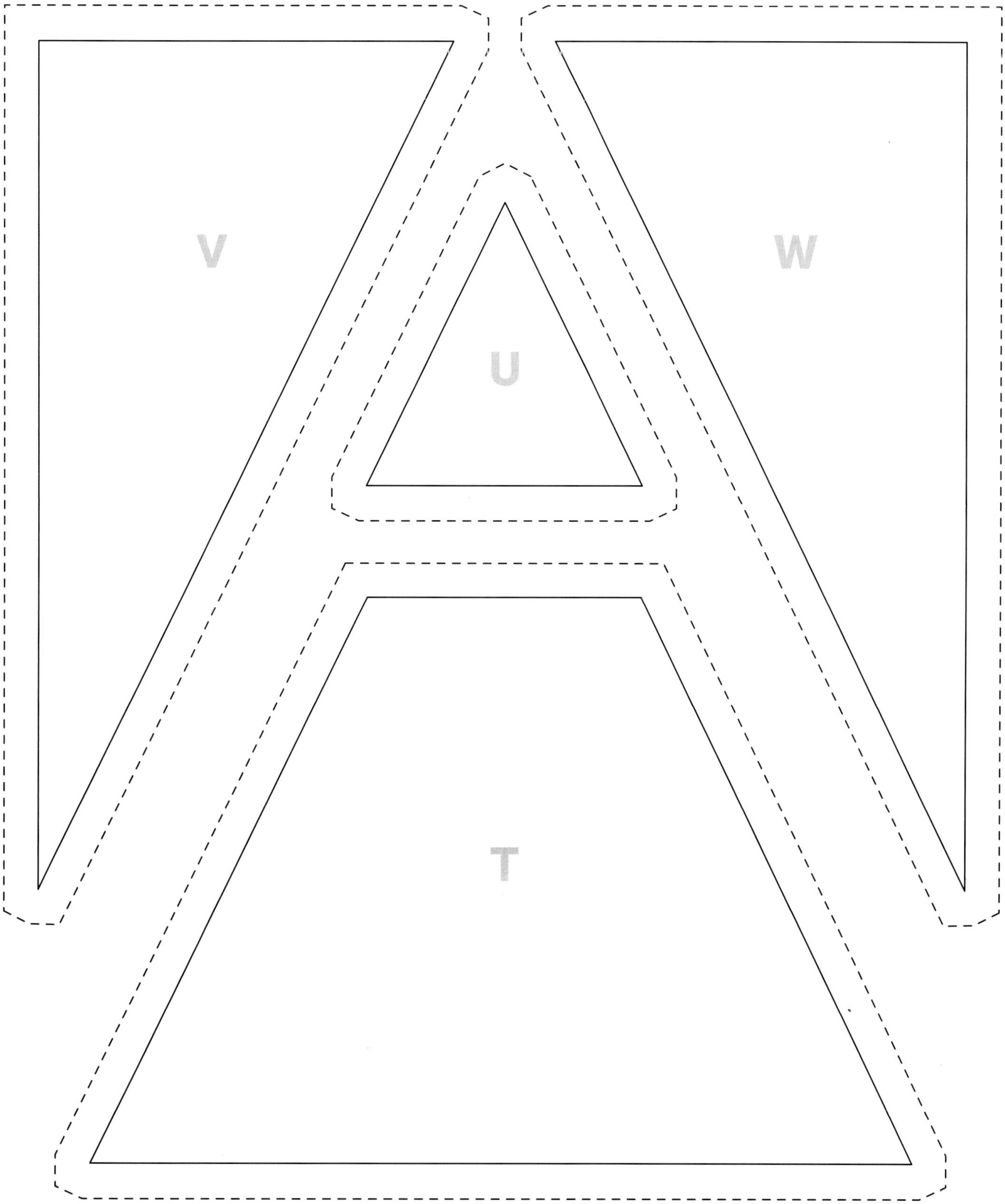
V
W
U
T

ACKNOWLEDGMENTS

To husband Mike and daughter Caitlyn: Thank you for standing by me through late nights, missed moments, and creation after creation. Your belief in me, your celebrations of each completed step along the way, and your love carried me through this process more than you know. And of course, thank you for your willingness to literally be seen in this book as models. We live in a house filled with love and quilts. Many, many quilts. But even more love.

To Allison Adams: Thank you for coming on the creative journey of quilt photography with me. I have learned so much from you, from light sources and photo manipulation to who has the best fan fold of a quilt (you do!) I am so grateful to have worked on this project together and grown in both friendship and skillsets. When I say "craaaazzy Alli," it is said with delight and affection.

To my Therapist: Though you shall remain unnamed for both of our sakes, it is only with your continued guidance that I was able to tackle a project of this magnitude once again. You helped me maintain my sanity as I dove headlong into this large project and became my biggest cheerleader along the way. Thank you for helping me see the ways that I have grown and what is still left to do. You said once that I only needed to thank myself for this book, and that was when I knew that I needed to actually thank you instead.

Scotch

INDEX

ABOUT THE AUTHOR

I am a 40s-something wife and mom, winding my way between family life and fabric. I've been sewing for as long as I can remember, and even did various super cool things such as making my own prom dress, a quilt for my college dorm room, and even my flower girl dresses. Well, those things *might* be cool now, but they definitely weren't then.

I create independent sewing patterns, including the best-selling Book Nerd pattern, available at my website, *angelapingel.com*. I have filmed a DVD on sewing curves, available through Quilting Arts, and also have a class on Craftsy, using precuts to make disappearing blocks. I have been published in numerous magazines and books including *Modern Blocks; Sweet Celebrations; Playful Little Paper-Pieced Projects; Quiltmaker's 100 Blocks, Vol. 5; 101 Patchwork Projects; Modern Patchwork Magazine; Quilt Scene Magazine*; and more.

You can find me sharing even more thoughts on my current projects on my website and through my fun newsletter, *Frayed Around the Edges*. And of course, please look for me on the social media of your choice under the name @angelapingel.

I currently reside in South Bend, IN, (Go Irish!) and can be found either in my sewing room, driving my daughter to and from dance, or reading yet another book. I'm lucky enough to have a husband who enjoys cooking and crafting a cocktail.